WHEN MINNEHAHA FLOWED WITH WHISKEY

When Minnehaha Flowed with Whiskey

A SPIRITED HISTORY OF THE FALLS

KAREN E. COOPER

MINNESOTA
HISTORICAL
SOCIETY PRESS

mnhspress.org

The Minnesota Historical Society Press is a member of the Association of University Presses.

Unless otherwise credited, all photographs are from the collection of the author; photographers' names are provided when known. Other image credits refer to the Hennepin History Museum (HHM), to the Hennepin County Library (HCL), and to the Minnesota Historical Society (MNHS).

Manufactured in the United States of America

10 9 8 7 6 5 4 3 2 1

∞ The paper used in this publication meets the minimum requirements of the American National Standard for Information Sciences—Permanence for Printed Library Materials, ANSI Z39.48–1984.

International Standard Book Number
ISBN: 978-1-68134-226-9 (paper)
ISBN: 978-1-68134-227-6 (e-book)

Library of Congress Control Number: 2022933905

This and other Minnesota Historical Society Press books are available from popular e-book vendors.

When Minnehaha Flowed with Whiskey is typeset in Wolpe Pegasus, a typeface originally designed and called Pegasus by Berthold Wolpe in 1937. The design was updated and revived by Toshi Omagari in 2017. Book design by Wendy Holdman.

To Henry, Anna, Clara, Ayla, and Matilda

Contents

Introduction:
The Lay of the Land

WHEN I GIVE A WALKING TOUR or a talk on Minnehaha's rowdy history, I am often met by an eager audience who promise lots of questions. That's a pleasing prospect, and one that pretty often disappoints me. It's my own fault. I tell a *thorough* story, and before the end of my hour, I will have answered pretty much every question people think along the way, and a few dozen more that no one besides me has ever asked.

Readers, you have in your hands a similarly conscientious effort. And it would be perfect, to my admittedly enthusiastic way of thinking, for this book to answer every question anyone might have about the history of Minnehaha Falls.

That's not possible. I haven't been able to answer all of my own questions, let alone yours. Instead, I am putting forth the history of whiskey, drinking, and mayhem at the falls, with occasional side trips to present some unusual and pertinent stories I've discovered along the way.

It all starts with the falling water. About six miles south of downtown Minneapolis, and squeezed in between Highway 55 and the Mississippi River, is a delightful surprise. Who would expect to find a perfect gem of a waterfall in a mostly flat prairie city? The ground under the city explains the waterfall, cascading as it does over layers of rock. Around 450 million years ago, an ocean with a sandy floor covered this southeastern part of today's Minnesota. That sand became the St. Peter sandstone layer of our local geology. That ocean had lots of mollusks and similar life forms in it; their shells fell to the ocean floor atop the sand and created a layer of Platteville limestone. Time and pressure turned these into layers of rock.[1]

The sandstone layer crumbles easily; moving water erodes it far more quickly than the limestone layer. Water enters the scene in a big way perhaps twelve thousand years ago, when glacial melt formed a body of water many miles to the northwest, hundreds of feet deep and far larger than today's Minnesota. A glacial moraine—a ridge of rock and sand—was high enough to hold back this lake, but eventually the water overtopped it and catastrophically poured downstream.

This massive flow of water scoured out the channel of the Minnesota River. The great draining of the glacial lake explains why the Mendota Bridge at the mouth of the Minnesota is three-quarters of a mile from bluff top to bluff top. That enormous valley carries a river less than two hundred feet wide. The flood of water that filled the valley was tremendously powerful, clearing away all sediment on top of the Platteville limestone and creating a massive waterfall called the River Warren Falls. This original post-glacial waterfall was located about where downtown St. Paul is today on the Mississippi.

Water eroded the sandstone under the limestone. Unsupported, the edge of the waterfall broke off. The great waterfall retreated upstream over thousands of years. It split at the confluence of the Mississippi and the Minnesota Rivers, and split again at the confluence of the Mississippi and Minnehaha Creek. Sandstone eroded away, limestone fell: this is clear and obvious at Minnehaha Falls, where there is a shallow cavern in the sandstone under the waterfall and blocks of limestone are found at the base of the falls.

Minnehaha Creek below the falls is a bit like the Minnesota River valley, flowing as it does between two high bluffs. The scale is cozier, of course. On days when the wind blows strongly, the air can be calm at creek level. In the post-glacial epoch, when plants, animals, and people came to live here, the Minnehaha gorge was an inviting environment, both practical and beautiful. Many kinds of nuts, berries, and other food plants grow along the creek, there would always have been deer and fish, and there might have been otters.[2]

A small archeological survey was done at Minnehaha in 2009–10, downstream from the falls, and it provides the earliest evidence of people in this beautiful place. Under the all-pervasive layer of modern trash, archaeologists found a couple of tiny pieces of pottery and some stone artifacts. These come from a few thousand years ago, when Indigenous people built hundreds of mounds in the area for

Minnehaha Falls, about 1880. The men stand on the sandstone layer; limestone looms overhead. A wooden footpath to the left of the falls was removed in the 1880s as collapsing limestone made the footing increasingly treacherous. *Photo by Charles Zimmerman*

burial, ceremonial, and religious purposes. White people building the cities destroyed most of these; Mounds Park, on the bluff above Wakan Tipi (Dwelling Place of the Sacred, Carver's Cave), in St. Paul, preserves a few of them.[3]

Closer in time to today, for many of the native Mdewakanton

Dakota people, the area at the confluence of the Mississippi and Minnesota Rivers is their place of origin: Bdote. The waters of Minnehaha Falls flow into the Mississippi and thence to the confluence, and they are part of Bdote—as are other places between Owamniyomni (Whirlpool, St. Anthony Falls) in downtown Minneapolis and Wakan Tipi just downstream from downtown St. Paul. One Dakota elder described the sacred and medicinal power of water: "We use water for healing, for purifying, for cleansing; we honor water. It's sacred to us. [In] all our ceremonies we use water and we pray with it. . . . That's what works; when you speak to the spirit of the water, it will make an end to anything you wish, cleansing, purifying. Water is powerful."[4]

~

Throughout the decades that Europeans have been in Minnesota, their place-names have been bestowed and sometimes changed. For sake of the narrative, I use current names. Thus, I have used "Fort Snelling" as the name for that place, even when it was first known as Fort St. Anthony. I use "Minnehaha Falls" and "Minnehaha Creek" when writing about early years when these were called "Little" or "Brown's." I use the current name for Bde Maka Ska, even when I am writing about the lake well before its original name was restored; the military had renamed it Lake Calhoun by the 1830s. In the case of the railroad past the falls, I elide the continual name changes into the "Milwaukee Road."

As for the name of the waterfall itself, Minnehaha does not mean "laughing waters." The name comes from the Dakota words for water (mni) and curling (ġaġa). It describes the water curling over the rock of the waterfall's edge. With its aspirated gs, "mniġaġa" sounds enough like "Mini-ha-ha" that English speakers allowed their imaginations to make the connection and used the word for waterfall to name these falls.

The waterfall is just three miles upstream from where the Mississippi and Minnesota Rivers meet. At that confluence, European-descended Americans established Fort Snelling. And so it is at Fort Snelling that the story of whiskey, mayhem, and Minnehaha begins.[5]

1

"Westward the Jug of Empire Takes Its Way"

MINNEHAHA FALLS IS TWO MILES—as the crow flies—north of the confluence of the Mississippi and Minnesota Rivers and the site of Fort Snelling. When the US Fifth Infantry arrived here in 1819, they came to build a fort to serve government interests on the Upper Mississippi. They traveled in keelboats and brought all the tools and supplies they needed—including plenty of whiskey. The soldiers were infamously hard drinkers; moreover, whiskey was vital to the government effort to take the land from the tribes who lived on it. From its beginning, Fort Snelling was an inebriated, drunken outpost, and that spilled over to nearby Minnehaha.

THE PEN OF HISTORY, DIPPED IN A WELL OF WHISKEY

The army post was intended to secure the lands of the Upper Mississippi for the United States, driving out the British fur traders who were trading with the Native hunters and trappers, extracting furs from land the United States felt it owned—they'd just paid France for the tract called Louisiana. Those furs were being shipped to Europe without taxes being paid on them, and the United States needed that tax income.

Lieutenant Zebulon Pike had, only a few years before, undertaken an expedition to the area. In 1805, he persuaded two local Dakota leaders to sign an agreement allowing the United States to build the post. The Dakota people's relationship with the land did not include considering the land as property; likely they understood that this agreement would allow use of the land and bring them easier access to trade goods.[1]

The United States, however, had a deliberate strategy for taking Native land. If Native nations were indebted, the tribes could be forced to sell their land in order to satisfy their debts. The fur trade gave Native people access to industrial products such as guns or traps, access to liquor, and access to items like cloth, cooking pots, and sewing needles. Hunters gathered furs during the winter when the pelts were thickest. Each man would begin the season provided with traps and guns. In the spring, the hunter returned with pelts and paid his debts. As the numbers of fur-bearing animals dropped, the trade could not sustain every hunter, and debts grew. Native people became more reliant on these trade goods; when the game in the area could not sustain families, they ceded land, gaining promises of annuity payments at the same time they paid the debts claimed by the traders. And alcohol was an important component of creating trading partnerships.[2]

Alcohol eased the relationship between a trader and the Native people who did business with him. At twenty-five cents a gallon, whiskey was much cheaper than beer or wine; because it was strong drink, it was economical to transport by the barrel. And everyone, Natives and non-Natives, wanted it. Drinking was the national pastime. It is simply staggering how much white Americans drank in the early 1800s. From morning until night, men, women, and even small children drank alcohol. They had beer, cider, wine, and whiskey; they drank at breakfast, at designated drink breaks during the workday, at dinner, and before bed. From 1790 to 1810, the number of distilleries in America grew to fourteen thousand operations—one for every fifty people. By the 1830s, at the peak of our national drunken stupor, Americans consumed the equivalent of seven gallons of grain alcohol per person per year. (Today we drink about a third of that.)[3]

The army was made up of particularly heavy drinkers. Every man's daily ration of whiskey was a gill: four fluid ounces, or half a cup, which meant an annual supply of eleven gallons of whiskey for every soldier. And they could purchase up to two gills more per day. As George Washington had said: "There should always be a sufficient quantity of spirits with the army, to furnish moderate supplies to the troops . . . such as when they are marching in hot or cold weather, in camp in wet, on fatigue or in working parties, it is so essential that it is not to be dispensed with." They were, to be sure, a mostly drunken bunch.[4]

In August 1819, the soldiers arrived at the confluence to build the fort on what they saw as empty land. They had their tools and supplies, which included barrels of whiskey. They arrived with just weeks to build shelter to survive the coming cold weather. After a torturous, disease-plagued winter, they commenced more construction on barracks and storehouses. A sawmill was needed, and they investigated Minnehaha Creek for its waterpower. But then and now, Minnehaha is a seasonal waterfall, and in the summer of 1820, the water was simply too low to power a mill. They built their mill at St. Anthony, reliable but inconveniently far away. Good, plentiful timber was found even farther north, floated down the Rum River to the Mississippi, and sawed at the government mill. (Dakota speakers call this Wakpa Waḳaŋ, Spirit River; those who named it the Rum River were English-speaking fur traders.) Two years later, the soldiers also built a grist mill at St. Anthony Falls. These new enterprises meant the soldiers also had to build a bridge across Minnehaha Creek so they

A photo taken in about 1866 shows the first part of the built environment at Minnehaha: the bridge across the creek on the road between St. Anthony Falls and Fort Snelling. Behind it is the larger railroad bridge, built in about 1865. The zigzag fence was on the edge of Franklin Steele's Little Falls Farm. Four guys court danger at the lip of the falls. *Photo by R. W. Ransom*

could easily traverse the seven miles between the fort and the mills. Through all their hard, hard work, the soldiers certainly cherished the relief they got from whiskey.

FORT SNELLING WAS A MAGNET: EVERYONE WAS DRAWN TO IT

Fort Snelling's first commander was Lieutenant Colonel Henry Leavenworth; after a year he was replaced by Colonel Josiah Snelling. Among the command was a Virginian, Major Lawrence Taliaferro (pronounced "Tolliver"), who had been appointed by President James Monroe to represent the United States to the Native nations of the area. Though Taliaferro was an army officer, he was not included in the fort's military organization. His job was Indian agent. He licensed the traders who dealt with the Native people, and he was diligent in trying to keep liquor and distilling operations from entering Native lands. Taliaferro had the power to remove trespassers on Native lands—by military force, if necessary—and he could and did negotiate between warring tribes. He also arrested and tried Natives who had been accused of crimes, and made sure the payments and annuities due to the tribes were delivered to them.

Taliaferro was a conscientious officer who was well aware of his duties as Indian agent. In those early months, when the first troops lived in a temporary camp at Coldwater Spring, he had harsh words about the fort's commander: "The first murder of one Indian by another, was caused by the giving of a bottle of whiskey to the old 'White Buzzard,' by Colonel Leavenworth at Cold Water Camp, which produced some very sharp correspondence between the commanding officer and the Indian agent." To Leavenworth, Taliaferro asserted the authority that came with his job, saying: "I beg, therefore, that no whiskey whatever be given to any Indians, unless it be through their proper agent. While an overplus of whiskey thwarts the beneficent and humane policy of the government, it entails misery upon the Indians, and endangers their lives." Taliaferro used alcohol to influence tribal leaders and gain their trust. He was charged with controlling the amount of alcohol available to them, and he was wary about the ill effect of providing too much.[5]

Though Fort Snelling was built on Dakota land, Ojibwe people from the north and east and Ho-Chunk people from the east and south were frequent visitors. Snelling had the soldiers build a council house, and Taliaferro used it for receiving delegations of Native people who came to receive annual diplomatic gifts and lodge complaints about fur traders. After the horrific experience of seeing a Native man get murdered over whiskey that Leavenworth had given to him, Lawrence Taliaferro was relieved to be in a new working relationship with Snelling. The two men were like-minded, and Taliaferro was able to set up and sometimes even enforce his strict regulations about providing whiskey to the Indigenous people.

As Indian agent for this new territory, Taliaferro was in charge of licensing the traders, both those working for the American Fur Company and the independents. One of the independent traders in the area was Benjamin F. Baker. He had come to Fort Snelling to be a teacher, but quickly entered the fur trade. Baker was well liked by the fort officials and became well established. In the 1820s he built a fine stone home and trading post at Coldwater, a spring about a mile northwest of the fort and a mile south of Minnehaha Falls. Many people started calling the area Baker's Settlement.[6]

In the 1820s, a group of refugees from the Red River Colony five hundred miles to the north arrived at Fort Snelling. In 1811 Lord Thomas Douglas, fifth Earl of Selkirk, a Scotsman and a major shareholder in the Hudson's Bay Company, had established a colony of poor Scottish farmers on the Red River in what is now Winnipeg, Manitoba. Some skilled tradesmen from Switzerland arrived in 1821, took a look around at the starving misery of the colonists, and decided not to stay. At the time, an American fur trader was at the colony, having driven a herd of cattle north, and he was about to return to Fort Snelling. Five families followed him, and by 1826, most of the Swiss had left the colony. Fort Snelling was far away, but there was nowhere else to go.

Most of these Selkirk refugees continued on to Galena, Illinois, or to St. Louis or even farther south. In the 1820s, it was illegal for anyone to settle on Native lands in what is now Minnesota, and Taliaferro enforced the law. The military reservation around the fort was the only land west of the Upper Mississippi River that Native tribes had ceded to the American government. Snelling permitted those who had skills needed by traders or the army to stay near the fort;

many ended up on the military reservation, near Baker's Settlement at Coldwater Spring. These squatters used and improved the land in hopes of being permitted to buy it when that became possible. Abraham Perret's family was eagerly welcomed; Mary Ann Perret was a skilled midwife, and the officers' wives insisted that she be permitted to stay. Other Selkirk refugees who stayed worked to raise and sell foodstuffs to the garrison, did blacksmithing on traps and other hardware, or became traders either independently or with the American Fur Company.[7]

SOLDIERS IN THEIR CUPS

The US Army's recruits were a motley mix of soldiers who had fought for the British in recent wars, as well as convicts and immigrants. Snelling, complaining about the quality of his command, said that "whiskey is their god and mutiny is their watchword." He requested a better class of men from his superiors, specifically citing an attack on the Dakota leader Little Crow by drunken soldiers and noting his frustration that "our martial code does not give me the power to punish these outrages in the principal manner which is best adapted to Indian customs, and I must either transcend the limits of the law or send our friendly neighbors away discontented." Snelling's frustration with the class of men who joined up was matched by that of other officers, and it foreshadows the class divisions that would eventually cause a war at Minnehaha.[8]

The difficulties with recruits were blamed on whiskey. Congress in the early nineteenth century spent much time on the problem of their drunken army. "Whiskey is not essential to the health of the soldier," argued a congressional committee considering ending the whiskey ration in 1830. "It is believed that drunkenness operates more extensively than all other causes combined in producing insubordination, desertion, disease and death, among our troops. Could their passion for stimulants be suppressed, their moral, intellectual, and physical condition would be incalculably improved, and a better class of our citizens would be induced to enter into the Army."[9]

Army Adjutant General R. Jones argued against the whiskey ration for soldiers: "If the soldier has acquired some taste for alcoholic drink previously to enlistment, which is the case with a majority, the practice of administering to him half a gill of whiskey twice every day most probably confirms the habit. If the recruit joins the service with an unvitiated [uncontaminated] taste, which is not unfrequently the case, the daily privilege and the uniform example soon induce him to taste and then to drink his allowance. The habit being presently acquired, he too soon becomes an habitual toper."[10]

And yet, the army officers had no clear idea how to solve this problem. They considered offering coffee, sugar, molasses, or money in exchange for the daily booze ration, but they also understood that the men wouldn't tolerate being forced to give it up.

While some army posts had great problems with deserters, those serving at Fort Snelling didn't really have anywhere to go. During the long months of winter isolation, drinking and playing cards were the easy solutions to the boredom of garrison life. Enlisted men were then permitted their gill of liquor a day but could easily get more. Officers had even easier access to liquor than the enlisted men, and there were no limits on their drinking. It was understood among the gentlemanly that perpetual inebriation would not be tolerated, but courts-martial for drunkenness still happened frequently at all levels of the chain of command. The officers' "social habits" caused more than a few to end their days in disgrace and poverty.

On February 3, 1829, Secretary of War Peter Buell Porter submitted a report to the Committee on Military Affairs of the House of Representatives, titled "On the Expediency and Effective Use of Ardent Spirits in the Army." Surgeon General Joseph Lovell contributed a letter, noting:

Under the present excellent regulations of the sutling department, the soldier can obtain ardent spirits in but three ways: from his ration; from the sutler, on the written permission of his commanding officer; and from the innumerable host of hucksters who infest almost every military post, and who always constitute the advance of a detachment of the army, though pushed ever so far beyond the limits of civilization. That the intemperate habits of the soldier are sometimes commenced, and always confirmed, by the agency of those traders in iniquity, is notorious to every one connected with the army; and the records of our civil courts will furnish evidence of the lengths to which the officers have often carried their exertions to protect their men from this desolating evil.[i]

In the winter of 1823, rations ran short. The whiskey supply was in no danger, but the bread was moldy and inedible. As Ann Adams, a member of one of the Selkirk refugee families who lived that winter in the former Coldwater barracks, recalled: "Sometimes it seemed all they had was whiskey. . . . Intemperance, among both officers and men, was an almost universal thing, and produced deplorable effects." Snelling was obviously aware of the detriments of drinking, even as he was likely becoming an alcoholic himself, and he was not exempt from the lack of restraint. When one of his not-infrequent "convivial spells occurred, he would act furious and make a scene, flogging his men for committing the same offense."[11]

The soldiers knew that so much drink was harmful, and at times embraced religion as an alternative to constant drunkenness. Snelling and family were once nearly stranded and starving on the shores of Lake Pepin, trying to get home to the fort as the winter weather closed in. They survived, and in his gratitude, Snelling became quite religious (and with that, abstinent) for a short time afterward. But before long, as Ann Adams noted, the "conviviality and worldliness of garrison life" once again wore away his fervent gratitude at surviving. He wasn't the only one for whom and at least for a while it seemed the balance of life had drink on the one hand and religion on the other. Drink nearly always won out.[12]

Surprisingly often, and as far back as 1820, notable visitors provided the fort's officers with some distraction: government surveyors, expeditions, and the odd wealthy adventurer stopped by. Some of the latter wrote books that began publicizing the wonders of the Upper Mississippi. In 1835 the artist George Catlin, who traveled to Fort Snelling by steamboat, recognized the beauty of the area—and its potential for tourism. He popularized the idea of a "Fashionable Tour," via steamboat: the beauties of the area were now "made so easily accessible to the world, and the only part of [the far West] to which ladies can have access. I would recommend to all who have time and inclination to devote to the enjoyment of so splendid a Tour, to wait not, but make it while the subject is new, and capable of producing the greatest degree of pleasure." Affluent sightseers took his advice, and the pretty Minnehaha Falls, just two miles from the fort, was a must-see on the tour.[13]

JOSEPH R. BROWN AND MINNEHAHA

At the beginning of Snelling's command at the fort in 1820, a new batch of recruits arrived. Among them was a fifteen-year-old drummer and fifer named Joseph Renshaw Brown. This teenager would go on to become the most mythological person associated with Minnehaha Falls: that is, the person about whom infamous stories are still told that cannot be proved. Minnesotans love their history, and the stories of Joe Brown and Minnehaha are the stories that get repeated and asked about more than any others. These stories persist because their unprovable core is shrouded by enticingly plausible possibilities.

Though Joe Brown began his time in Minnesota as a mere musician in the military band, he would become one of Minnesota's most prominent white settlers. Brown's Valley and Brown County, both in Minnesota, are named for him. Minnehaha Falls, however, was not.

The earliest explorers, going back to Jonathan Carver in 1766, made no record of the pretty waterfall, even though most of them passed right by it.

But as the fort became more established, Minnehaha soon became a favorite destination for visitors. The waterfall's name was delightfully fluid between 1820 and 1840. Military maps sometimes called the place Brown's Falls, located right on Brown's Creek. The persistent myth is that both locations were named for Joe Brown, but that is not true. The name was actually bestowed in honor of General Jacob J. Brown, the commander who had ordered the Fifth Infantry to build what became Fort Snelling—and who became the army's highest-ranking officer soon after.[14]

In those early days, the other common name for the waterfall was the Little Falls. This was to differentiate it from St. Anthony Falls, six or seven miles up the Mississippi River. The "big falls" designation isn't about how tall either waterfall is. St. Anthony Falls, the only waterfall on the entire Mississippi, plunged a mere sixteen feet, less than a third of Minnehaha's drop. St. Anthony's superlative title instead stems from the fact that its waterpower comes from a mighty river whose watershed encompasses thousands of square miles, not the modest stream that outflows from a single—albeit large—lake that powers Minnehaha.[15]

The first known written description of Minnehaha Falls was by William H. Keating, who in 1823 accompanied Major Stephen H. Long to locate the international boundary between the United States and the British possessions to the north.

The country about the fort contains several other water falls, which are represented as worthy of being seen. One of them, which is but two miles and a half from the garrison, and on the road to St. Anthony's, is very interesting. It is known by the name of Brown's Fall, and is remarkable for the soft beauties which it presents. Essentially different from St. Anthony's, it appears as if all its native wildness had been removed by the hand of art. A small, but beautiful stream, about five yards wide, flows gently until it reaches the verge of a rock, from which it is precipitated to a depth of forty-three feet, presenting a beautiful parabolic sheet, which drops without the least deviation from the regular curve, and meets with no interruption from neighbouring rocks, or other impediments, until it has reached its lower level, when it resumes its course without any other difference, than that produced by the white foam which floats upon its surface. The spray, which this cascade emits, is very considerable, and when the rays of the sun shine upon it, produces a beautiful Iris; upon the surrounding vegetation the effect of this spray is distinct; it vivifies all the plants, imparts to them an intense green colour, and gives rise to a stouter growth than is observed upon the surrounding country. On the neighbouring rock the effect is as characteristic, though of a destructive nature; the spray striking against the rock, which is of a loose structure, has undermined it in a curved manner, so as to produce an excavation, similar in form to a Saxon arch, between the surface of the rock and the sheet of water; under this large arch we passed with no other inconvenience than that which arose from the spray. There is nothing sublime or awfully impressive in this cascade, but it has every feature that is required to constitute beauty; it is such a fall as the hand of opulence daily attempts to produce in the midst of those gardens upon which treasures have been lavished for the purpose of imitating nature; with this difference, however, that these falls possess an easy grace destitute of the stiffness which generally distinguishes the works of man from those of nature. The stream that exhibits this cascade falls into the Mississippi about two miles above the fort; it heads in a lake situated a few miles above. A body of water, which is not represented upon any map that we know of, has been discovered in this vicinity within a few years, and has received the name of Lake Calhoun, in honour of the Secretary at War. Its dimensions are small. Another lake of a much larger size is said to have been discovered about thirty or forty miles to the north-west of the fort. Its size, which is variously stated, is by some supposed to be equal to that of Lake Champlain, which, however, from the nature of the country and the knowledge which we have of the course of the rivers, appears scarcely possible.[ii]

An oft-told story about Joe Brown and Minnehaha Falls involves that large lake, Minnetonka. Brown had become friends with Colonel Snelling's son, Will, and in May of 1822 the two boys, along with Samuel Watkins and a youngster with the surname Stewart, went exploring upstream in Minnehaha Creek until they reached the lake that is the source of Minnehaha Falls. No white person had left a record of seeing it before. They were gone two nights, camping the second night "on the big island in the second lake." It's a fun story, and it may even be true.[16]

Joe Brown has often been called the first settler of Hennepin County, due to the fact that he supposedly made a claim at the mouth of Minnehaha Creek in 1826. This story seems to have originated thirty years after the fact in a public lecture by John H. Stevens called "The Early History of Hennepin County," and the story has been repeated many times since.[17]

But if Brown made a claim at the mouth of Minnehaha Creek in 1826, it would have been no more legal than those of the Selkirk squatters who continued to congregate at Baker's Settlement at the Coldwater Spring. Like those squatters, Brown required permission from Colonel Snelling to settle on the military reservation. Staking a claim on the military reservation was no guarantee of getting the land later on. In addition, soldiers were not allowed to claim land because, being in the service, they couldn't fulfill the government requirement that they live on and improve the land until it was surveyed and offered for sale. Stevens said Brown made no improvements to the land, which would have been a vital step in making a claim, and he reported that Brown gave up the claim in 1830, decades before he could have legally purchased it.[18]

Some parts of Brown's life story are easier to prove, including some atrocious behavior he engaged in which set the stage for future hijinks at Minnehaha Falls.

By 1828, Joe Brown had left the army and entered the fur trade, taking posts on rivers south of today's Minnesota (and was obviously not living on a claim at Minnehaha). With a couple of years' experience, he became a clerk to Alexis Bailly at Mendota. He was likely at Hastings, Minnesota, in the summer of 1831. The place was then called Oliver's Grove and was a known drop-off point for

The unceasing demand for alcohol inspired some to cook up home brew. One such brewer, Hannibal, was an enslaved man purchased in 1833 in St. Louis by Major John Bliss, the fort's commander from 1833 to 1836. Bliss's son, John H. Bliss, recorded this memory of Hannibal in the 1890s. The "black hole" was a windowless solitary confinement cell in the guard house. "Catching a good licking" may have meant Hannibal was whipped.

Hannibal . . . was a most excellent and faithful fellow. The only difficulty I remember his getting into was brewing spruce beer and selling it to the soldiers. Everything in this line was among the prerogatives of our sutler, Mr. Myrie, who made complaint to my father, who admonished Hannibal that this was outside the line of his duties. He made promise of amendment, but was soon caught at it again, which resulted in his catching a good licking and forty-eight hours' confinement in the black hole, effecting a thorough reformation.[iii]

alcohol being smuggled to traders deeper in the country. Bailly and Brown set themselves up for an intense season of competition with the American Fur Company, their erstwhile employer. Using capital from New York for their enterprise, they hired as many experienced traders as they could, undercut the American Fur Company traders on prices, and used what Brown's biographers refer to as "a considerable quantity of whiskey" to convince the Native people to trade with them. Their collaboration eventually fell through in 1832, when they lost their eastern capital, but Brown still had his eye out for a way to make his fortune.[19]

He knew whiskey was the key ingredient. America had finally begun to address its problem with its staggering drunkenness in the 1830s. In 1832, the army stopped its daily whiskey ration. This did nothing to decrease demand: soldiers happily jumped the walls to find booze at nearby trading posts. Around the same time, the government increased restrictions on transporting alcohol on the frontier. From his time in the army, Brown was intimately familiar with the rigors of garrison life. He knew how keenly the soldiers were interested in drink. And he had long experience with sneaking alcohol into areas where it was forbidden. Trading furs for goods and whiskey was one route to profit. But true frontiersmen never settled for just one route, and Brown soon came up with an idea that would turn him into a thorn in the side of the fort's officials.

He called it Rum Town, though some people just called it The Hell.

WHISKEY: SUPPLY, DEMAND, AND PANDEMONIUM

Brown's new business opened in 1838, a turbulent time. Major changes were coming to the confluence. In 1837, the US government forced the signing of the "White Pine Treaty" with the Ojibwe, which opened land east of the Mississippi to settlement. This included a large area of valuable timberland in the St. Croix valley, where entrepreneurs were already cutting down the forest. The army saw looming threats: more squatters on its military reservation, more grogshops, more competition for scarce wood. Major Joseph Plympton, the commander of the fort from 1837 to 1841, ordered a survey to establish the formal boundaries of the reservation.

The work of defining the reservation included a census of the settlements outside the fort at Coldwater Spring and across the river. The survey counted 157 people living on the reservation outside the fort, with 82 of them living near Coldwater. For some time, all those squatters had been causing problems, sometimes expensive problems, for the army and for Indian agent Taliaferro. Taliaferro had the responsibility to make good on what he called "sometimes fictitious" stock losses: those who lost cattle to hungry and resentful Dakota hunters made claims for payment, which claims were sometimes just little scams run on the government by the squatters and traders.[20]

The proposed new reservation boundaries included Rum Town, the fur post at Mendota, and good chunks of land along the Minnesota and Mississippi Rivers, effectively removing the whiskey sellers' proximity to their customers. But the people living at Coldwater and on the riverbanks outside the fort believed that they had a preemptive right to those lands. In some cases, they had lived there for ten or more years, they had made improvements, and they supplied the garrison with food or did other work for the army. Some of them were accused of whiskey peddling. They lodged protests as Major Plympton awaited the Senate's ratification of the 1837 treaty and the approval of the new boundaries.[21]

This is how matters stood in 1839, when Brown opened a grogshop on the east bank of the Mississippi River. About twenty-five people were squatting there in those early days, and some would soon be his employees. The steamboat *Ariel* brought twenty barrels of whiskey upriver to stock the grogshop. The post's surgeon, Dr. John Emerson, recorded that Brown was building a very extensive whiskey shop within gunshot of the fort, and on the military reserve. Even earlier, throughout the winter, the surgeon noted that the post was "completely inundated with ardent spirits and consequently the most beastly scenes of intoxication among the soldiers . . . and Indians" and that Brown was responsible for all of it.[22]

Brown had hired a man named Henry C. Mencke (pronounced "Mink") to run the saloon for him, and he was markedly successful. After one notable booze-up on June 3, 1839, a full two-thirds of the fort's soldiers found themselves in the lockup for drunkenness. Matters escalated. Unknown parties (Brown thought they were noncommissioned officers and French Canadians) wrecked the place in June. In September, Mencke was visited by fifteen or twenty Dakota men who wanted to buy whiskey. The manager knew this would violate his license to trade. He refused, leading the Dakota to steal a few gallons of whiskey and start to tear off the roof.

Outnumbered, Mencke ran to the fort for help. Plympton shrugged, telling him that Taliaferro was the one who handled "Indian matters." As it happened, Taliaferro was not home, but his interpreter went over the river to look into the situation. Of course, by that time the vandals had dispersed.

Taliaferro explained the Native men's behavior by saying that they were scheduled to receive their government annuity payment soon and so "some of the braves in order to prevent great drunkenness and bloodshed among their people proceeded without consultation except among themselves to break up the establishment." It's a story that changed over time. By October, he claimed that it was all "the acts of drunken Indians" and implied that the amount of whiskey taken was gallons more than first reported.

Brown decided to take direct legal action against Taliaferro. He sent his agents (Mencke and another one of his employees, an east-side squatter named Clewet) downriver to the nearest court that held jurisdiction over the area. Brown also let the Dakota know that they were responsible for his losses and the damage to his shop. Their leader, Red Hail, told Taliaferro and others in council that the restitution money would have to be paid from their pockets; it could not be deducted from the expected annuities. Red Hail spoke directly to Taliaferro and Plympton, the leaders at the fort. He said Taliaferro's interpreter had given him money to go across the river to Brown's grogshop and get the whiskey. (Of course, Taliaferro denied knowing anything about that.) "You told me to drive him off," said Red Hail, "so if anything comes of it you must pay your money and not ours."

Mencke, meanwhile, had been made a special deputy by the sheriff who maintained jurisdiction on the east side of the river where the grogshop was located. Clewet swore out a warrant against Taliaferro, then he and Mencke carried it over to the fort. Early in the morning of October 5, they burst into Taliaferro's house, threw him out of bed, put a pistol to his head, and announced that he was under arrest for trespass and damages.

Because Taliaferro hadn't trespassed into the grogshop himself, Mencke's legal argument was on shaky ground, but that hardly mattered. Mencke held Taliaferro at gunpoint for hours and refused to take bail money from anyone but him. After nine hours and many attempts by Dr. Emerson to end the standoff, Plympton finally sent over a detachment of soldiers from the fort to rescue the Indian agent. Because he had military authority, Taliaferro then had Mencke escorted back to the river's east bank. He had a stronger legal argument when he pointed out that Mencke happened to be an Englishman and was therefore "in Indian country without a passport."

The efforts to clear the military reservation had been creaking along. In October 1839, after the US Senate ratified the 1837 treaty and the military accepted the new boundaries, the secretary of war ordered the squatters (the "non-military personnel") to leave the military reservation by May 1840. Some left, but some refused, and so a detachment of soldiers was ordered to remove the belongings from the settlers' cabins, and then to burn them to the ground. The settlers moved off downriver—far enough to be outside the military reservation—to the eventual site of St. Paul. Joe Brown turned his attention to another grogshop, this one along the St. Croix.

∼

In the late 1830s, Franklin Steele came to the confluence of the rivers. It was Steele who began to see that adding hospitality to the famous Minnehaha Falls would likewise add to his sources of income. Eventually, this "hospitality" turned Minnehaha into a scene of drunken debauchery. It was Steele who set those wheels in motion.

The grandson of Scots immigrants to Pennsylvania, Steele had married well. The grandfather of his wife, Annie Barney, had signed the Declaration of Independence, and other members of her family had served in the navy in the Revolutionary War and the War of 1812. Steele's own family was made up of army officers who had served in both wars and in Pennsylvania's state government. He came from prosperous and respected people—he said his occupation was "gentleman"—and he proved himself capable of creating wealth and prosperity. Steele first turned up on the Minnesota frontier in 1837 with $1,000 in his pocket and an eye for profitable circumstances, which he quickly spotted. He staked a claim on the east side of Taylors Falls, in the just-ceded pine-

Franklin Steele,
about 1856. *MNHS*

lands. In a year, Steele parlayed his initial thousand-dollar investment into $13,000, and then used that to buy the sutler's store at Fort Snelling, an operation he ran for twenty years.[23]

The newly defined military reservation at the confluence included some land on both sides of the Mississippi. It also included the falls at St. Anthony. This waterfall was the most commercially important place in all of Minnesota because this waterpower would power the mills that built the economy of Minneapolis. When legal claims were initially made available, Steele was famously first on the spot on the east bank at St. Anthony Falls. He was sleeping on a pile of hay inside a very rough claim cabin when fort commander Joseph Plympton arrived, intending to claim the waterpower of the falls for himself. Plympton had drawn the reservation boundaries not just to shut down Brown's Rum Town and not just to chase away the squatters at Baker's Settlement. He meant to make that claim at St. Anthony. Steele held his claim against all comers. By 1847, using his connections back East, Steele had accumulated the capital he needed to fund the men and machinery necessary to start a sawmill operation. He hired Ard Godfrey, a millwright from Maine, to come out and supervise construction, and workers began cutting lumber by September of the following year.

THE ST. LOUIS HOTEL AT COLDWATER SPRING

In late 1839, Benjamin F. Baker had left his stone trading house at Coldwater. He was in St. Louis, dying. He turned his estate over to his old colleague, Kenneth McKenzie, a Canadian Scot who had gained American citizenship and become a successful fur trader. McKenzie had deep experience in the Minnesota area and in the use of whiskey. He was first licensed by Taliaferro to trade on the Minnesota River in the 1820s; in 1828 he left for the Missouri River, where he led the trade for John Jacob Astor's American Fur Company (AFC). When the government prohibited fur traders from using whiskey, McKenzie shipped upriver all the parts he needed to build a still. He then traded with local tribes for the grain he needed to make whiskey. He was justifiably proud of twisting the rules and chose to show off his still to a couple of visiting traders. As soon as they got back to St. Louis, they turned him in. The AFC nearly lost its license; McKenzie moved to St. Louis, and around 1834, he set up in business with some of the Chouteau family of fur traders. As Benjamin Baker lay dying, we don't know how McKenzie provided for Baker's Ojibwe wife and children and employees, but we know he kept his eye on the stone house at Coldwater.[24]

There was no rush to turn this property into a watering hole. Letting the ashes of the Coldwater settlement cool was probably a good idea. And so, expediently, missionary families moved in. For a few years, brothers Samuel and Gideon Pond rented half the house, while two families of Swiss missionaries rented the other half.[25]

The house eventually fell into disuse. In 1849, the year Minnesota Territory was established, author E. Sandford Seymour traveled to what he dubbed "the New England of the West" to write a book extolling the resources of the area, "which is destined to become one of the most flourishing States in the Union." Seymour's account of the area around Coldwater Spring, which he mistakenly called Rum Town, includes a description of a business opportunity: a "large, two-story stone house" that could not be occupied as it was on the military reservation. The veranda across the front of the house had partially collapsed, but Seymour could see that this place could provide a pleasant retreat for the "overtasked student," invalids, or "the man of pleasure in pursuit of amusement." The house had a barroom on the first floor, "the bar being protected by a strong partition, with a small hole left for the passage of the liquor." (This is the exact description of the illegal saloons that would so plague Minnehaha in the next many decades.)[26]

People began flooding into the new territory, seeking out business opportunities, and a few years later, McKenzie expanded Baker's old stone house with an addition, converting the place into the St. Louis Hotel, and several different men ran this business on his behalf through the years. McKenzie had it in operation at least from 1853 when it was "newly enlarged and improved and elegantly fitted up." McKenzie and sutler Franklin Steele were together in the business of stocking the hotel with fine champagne and brandy.[27]

The newcomers influenced the state's politics. With few exceptions, Protestant businessmen, often with Yankee roots, controlled the top levels of business and had disproportionate social influence.

These elites were behind the effort to make Minnesota a dry territory. In March 1852 the territorial legislature passed a "Bill for the Suppression of Drinking Houses and Tippling Shops," pending a public referendum on it; the law went into effect in May. Minnesota Territory had voted to go "dry." Its supporters were not the entirety of the population—of course they weren't. And the St. Louis Hotel figured in a protest.[28]

The place very likely was under Kenneth McKenzie's control when a scene of some revelry occurred on July 4, 1852: "Many of the citizens of St. Anthony, led by Al. Stone, attended a ball at the St. Louis House, near the cold springs, below Minnehaha Falls." Alvin Stone was a house painter, one of the patrons of the first and only tavern in St. Anthony: Alexis Cloutier's bowling saloon. Possibly Stone figured that because the stone house at Coldwater was on the military reservation, it was outside the immediate reach of the sheriff. This party was put together in response to the new law, which shut down Cloutier's saloon in June. After the "dry" referendum passed, tavern keeper Alexis Cloutier was sued for violating the law. Cloutier lost, but won on appeal, as the higher court found the prohibition referendum unconstitutional: nothing in law gave the public the right to legislate. It was not the powerful and elite businessmen who were the customers of tippling shops. The customers were the French Canadians and Irish and others who were foreign-born (and largely Catholic) and who comprised the working classes of Minnesota Territory.[29]

As the cities grew, foreign-born people became ever-more substantial segments of the population. The rift between the two groups—the native-born Protestants who accumulated wealth and social control and the immigrants who arrived with little and had scant access to capital—became entrenched in the way the community developed. The social stratification and unequal opportunity were to play out at Minnehaha Park—and are still with us today.

Though the "dry" bill passed 853–662 in the territory, more than half the "no" votes came from St. Paul. When the church bells rang in celebration, the Catholic bishop Joseph Crétin took some heat from his drink-loving parishioners. He was "genuinely shocked by the ravages caused on the frontier by whiskey, among Indians and whites alike," as historian Marvin O'Connell noted. In later years, the

A. G. McKenzie, who has not proved to be any relation to Kenneth McKenzie, ran this advertisement for the St. Louis House in 1856, in a pamphlet that reprinted a speech John Stevens delivered to the Minneapolis Lyceum. *HCL*

ST. LOUIS HOUSE.

A. G. McKENZIE, Proprietor.

THE location of this popular Hotel is distinguished in Minnesota history as being near Fort Snelling, on the bank of the Mississippi river, and is a desirable resort for pleasure seekers, or those who wish pleasant and agreeable retirement from the perplexities and cares of business for the purpose of recruiting enervated health. The new proprietor promises additional inducements to the public for a liberal patronage. 44tf

support for temperance continued under Bishop John Ireland, who was convinced, wrote O'Connell, that "the consumption of strong drink was a universal and unmitigated wickedness."[30]

As may be, people still drank. The St. Louis Hotel was a modest success for a few years, standing at Coldwater Spring on the road between Fort Snelling and Minnehaha Falls. In 1856, a man named A. G. McKenzie ran the place, and he bought some items for his operation from sutler Franklin Steele. A record in the Steele papers shows that from June to October, 1856, McKenzie spent nearly three times as much on alcohol as on foodstuff:

Flour	$8.50	Butter	$3.80
Coffee	$1.00	Sugar	$1.00
Soda	$0.38	Yeast Powder	$0.10
Veal	$2.63	Five gallons of Brandy	$30.00
Sugar	$1.00	1 Basket of Champagne	$22.00
Potatoes & corn	$0.80	"Drink"	$2.00[31]

The place burned down in the spring of 1860, but the loss to those looking to drink was not as great as it might have been. Franklin Steele invited the forces of merriment and mayhem to Minnehaha Falls.

2

The Long Tail of Longfellow

THE AREA BETWEEN FORT SNELLING and Minnehaha Falls had a thoroughly whiskey-soaked reputation by the late 1830s, when those taking the Fashionable Tour began arriving. By the mid-1850s, the forces of wealth and higher social class would make a greater claim to the area, a claim based on wealth creation but also firmly anchored in the highbrow realms of art and poetry. This cultural claim set up a dynamic at Minnehaha that persisted for sixty years.

Three historical streams came together in the 1850s to create the worldwide and lasting fame of Minnehaha Falls. One was the increasing reach of the railroads, which made it easier to consider taking an excursion to Minnesota Territory or perhaps moving there to build a future and a fortune. The second was Henry Wadsworth Longfellow's epic poem *The Song of Hiawatha*, which turned the falls into a location beloved by readers all over the world. But before either of those, there was the invention of photography.

Our intensely visual, image-based contemporary world means we can take for granted what is actually an extraordinary idea: we can know what something looks like even though we've never seen it in person. Before photography, painted and drawn images—whether good or bad—passed for real knowledge. But in 1839, a Frenchman named Louis Daguerre gave the world his image-making process. The daguerreotype, one of the earliest forms of photography, made its way across the Atlantic, and it took American artists just months to master and then improve on the art of making startlingly perfect images. From then on, absolutely astounding, world-changing visual representations became widely available, causing French painter Paul Delaroche to declare, "Painting is dead from this day forward."[1]

Daguerreotypes were made on a silver-plated, polished sheet of copper, which was coated with iodine vapor and then exposed to light in the camera. The latent image was then revealed by exposing the plate to hot mercury vapors; the mercury adhered to those parts of the plate most exposed to light, and not to darker, shadowed areas. This plate was washed in hyposulfite of soda and then distilled water. The result would be sealed under glass in a decorative case to protect the delicate chemical films on the silvered sheet and to prevent tarnishing.

These were not photographs; they did not have a negative. Instead, daguerreotypes were individual and unique artworks. Moreover, they were reversed images, "a reflecting mirror" of reality. The silvered, polished metal produced a highly reflective image which could only be seen when held at the correct angle. This mirror-like surface was indeed a drawback, but daguerreotypes were able to produce a minute perfection of accurate detail that was completely new in the visual arts. And they were dumbfounding to those seeing them for the first time.[iv]

The first photographic image ever taken of Minnehaha Falls was a daguerreotype. Such an image provides a benchmark, a visual data point, for all the changes that occurred at the falls as the decades went on. But the image is also significant because of the claim that Henry Wadsworth Longfellow used it as the inspiration for the poem that would make the falls of Minnehaha famous.

Spoiler alert: This is nonsense.

That claim was made by Alexander Hesler, a daguerreotypist from Galena, Illinois, a river town about 275 miles down the Mississippi from Minneapolis. Specifically, Hesler claimed that he took the first daguerreotype of Minnehaha Falls and sold it from his Galena studio to a man named George Sumner, who then brought it back to Cambridge, Massachusetts, and gave it to Longfellow. Most historians accept as authoritative Hesler's claim that he influenced Longfellow.[2]

Hesler's first point, that he took the first picture of the falls, seems to be true—that is, some of the details in his story are provable. In one of his tales, for example, he mentioned a man who had a land claim at the falls. Hesler was out taking images with his assistant, Joel Whitney, and they arrived at Minnehaha Falls:

Here after cutting down two trees we had an unobstructed
view and secured 25 or thirty pictures. While at work, a man
from the Emerald Isle, who had built a claim shanty just north
of the fall, discovered our [darkroom] tent and came up with
anger in his voice, and fire in his eye—exclaimed—"And what
air yees doing here jumping me claim."—After assuring him
that on the contrary we were only doing that which would
make the place famous and known over the civilized world,
with this explanation he became our obedient servant and
procured us a jug of cold water that flowed out of the rocks
at the foot of the fall on the South side.[3]

Hesler could not have expected that his image would make the
place world famous. But this man "from the Emerald Isle" was a real

A view by an unknown photographer, about 1867, shows the second bridge built
downstream from the falls. Note the stump: was that a tree Alexander Hesler and
Joel Whitney cut down? *Published by Collection L. L. Paris Vues d'Amerique*

person. His name was Patrick Maloney, and records show his 107-acre claim along the north side of the creek and right at the falls, which he paid for on October 1, 1855. In 1852, the land on the west side of the Mississippi River was still part of the military reservation, though Fort Snelling's commander was beginning to allow a small number of claims north of the creek.[4]

It seems that Hesler wrote this story in 1886 in an undated letter to Captain Russell Blakeley, a vice president of the Minnesota Historical Society who had spent his working life on the steamboats of the Upper Mississippi. Blakeley had surely met Hesler in the 1850s, when both men were in Galena, one learning the ropes of the steamboat trade, the other setting up a daguerreotype studio. By the 1880s, Hesler's picture-taking expedition and the publication of Longfellow's poem were thirty years in the past. Hesler had been telling and embellishing the story for decades. Like many of those who arrived early on, Blakeley was devoted to preserving early Minnesota history. He must have heard Hesler's story and asked him to preserve it.[5]

Hesler claimed several times that he took the first picture of Minnehaha Falls in 1851, but the evidence doesn't support this date. Letters from Hesler to photography journals in 1851 and 1852 show that he was indeed in Minnesota in both years. In early June 1851, he was taking "views" (as he referred to daguerreotype images), including images of St. Anthony Falls, for a never-published travel guide that *Harper's New Monthly* magazine was considering (and did publish, in a way, with their several articles on the Upper Mississippi in 1853 and later). He claimed more than once over the years that he took the first picture of Minnehaha Falls in August, often including the vivid detail that it was fearfully hot that day. But in mid-August 1851, when Hesler said he was in Minnesota, the temperature dropped 30 degrees in a day. Had he been in the state, he might have recalled such unusual weather. Climate records from 1852 show a string of days in August when the temperature was in the nineties.[6]

We can be confident, though, that Alexander Hesler took the first pictures of Minnehaha Falls in August 1852, using the daguerreotype process. No one else ever contradicted that claim or asserted that they had taken the first picture. Hesler's assistant that day was Joel E. Whitney, who became one of the most important early photographers in

Minnesota. Whitney never contradicted this story. It was a terribly hot day; Hesler spoke to an Irish man. That's all good evidence.

Hesler and Whitney were prepared to make dozens of exposures on that day. Their outing took them to St. Anthony Falls, Minnehaha, Fort Snelling, and Mendota. Any of those "25 or thirty" images Hesler claimed to make at Minnehaha Falls could be called the first photograph of the falls. And given how spectacular daguerreotype images were, and how famous the waterfall became quite soon after, they were probably cherished images.

An extensive search has turned up just four daguerreotypes of Minnehaha Falls. Two are in private collections (one on the East Coast and one in Minnesota) and two are in small museums (the Nelson-Atkins in Kansas City, Missouri, and the Chrysler in Norfolk, Virginia). None of those, however, have any provenance to show that they were taken by Hesler. There is no definitive thread that connects Alexander Hesler to any extant daguerreotype of the falls.

But what of Hesler's other claim? That his image was eventually given to Longfellow, who was inspired by it to write *The Song of Hiawatha*? That's a much more complicated claim, one that's much more difficult to prove—and one that has never yet been carefully examined.

In all of Longfellow's correspondence, which has been laboriously collected and published in six volumes, there is no hint that any Minnehaha Falls daguerreotype ever reached him. Longfellow certainly knew what a daguerreotype was. He and his family were "daguerred" on several occasions, and some of those images survive today. There is no Minnehaha daguerreotype in Longfellow's house, now a National Historic Site operated by the National Park Service. Neither his correspondence nor his journal mentions Hesler or George Sumner or an image of Minnehaha.[7]

Hesler claimed that Longfellow thanked him for the inspiring photograph by sending him a copy of *Hiawatha* in January 1856, just two months after the poem was published. In 1938, photography historian Robert Taft reported Hesler's daughter-in-law saying that the family still had this book, signed by the poet to the photographer. The inscription reads, "Mr. A. Hesler / With compliments / of the Author / Jany, 1856."[8]

Minnehaha Falls, about 1857. One of the four daguerreotypes of the falls that are known to still exist. *Chrysler Museum of Art, Norfolk, VA*

That inscription, of course, does not make Hesler's case.

The man who supposedly purchased and gave the daguerreotype to Longfellow was George Sumner. He was a noted intellectual, historian, and diplomat whose brother was Charles Sumner, the important abolitionist and senator from Massachusetts. Both Sumners were great friends of Longfellow. George Sumner left no major writings of his own, but Charles Sumner and Longfellow wrote letters constantly, and each was important enough that his letters were saved by others. These letters help to tell a story that differs from Hesler's.[9]

George Sumner returned to America in April of 1852 after living abroad for fourteen years. Through the rest of that year, he was in Cambridge, having meals with and visiting Longfellow. In August and early September, he also visited Charles in Washington and vacationed with Longfellow in Newport, Rhode Island. Hesler's claims that George Sumner was in Galena and carried a daguerreotype back to Longfellow in either 1851, when he was still abroad, or 1852, when he did not travel to the Mississippi, are false.[10]

Unlike the homebody Longfellow, George did travel to the Mississippi, however. As a respected public speaker who lectured regularly, he undertook his first lecture tour to the West in April 1853. He was in Madison, Wisconsin, on July 21. He could have traveled the ninety miles to Galena, but there is no proof either way. In the spring of 1854, Sumner gave a talk in Freeport, Illinois—one county east of Galena. Likely, George traveled to Freeport by stagecoach from Chicago. Maybe he continued a further fifty miles to Galena. If he made it to Galena, he could have visited Hesler's gallery, which was still there, though in a short time Hesler would move the gallery to Chicago. This is the thin, hypothetical journey supporting the possibility that George Sumner was ever in Galena, or that he could have purchased a daguerreotype of Minnehaha from Hesler.[11]

The story of Minnehaha Falls is nothing without coincidental occurrences and random-seeming tangents, and there is another potential vector for this transaction. In 1853 one of Hesler's daguerreotypes of Minnehaha Falls was shown in the Crystal Palace exhibit hall at the Exhibition of the Industry of All Nations in New York City. Hesler was in attendance; he later sold paper photographs of the interior of the Crystal Palace. If Hesler had claimed that George Sumner acquired the Minnehaha Falls daguerreotype while both were at the exhibition, that would be a completely believable story. But he always placed Sumner in Galena to collect the picture. Neither did Longfellow, as Hesler claimed, take to the woods to write the poem. He wrote *Hiawatha* in his own comfortable study, surrounded by books and pictures of loved ones.[12]

Hesler was an esteemed craftsman in the daguerreotype era. He won many awards for his work at the New York World's Fair, the

Wisconsin State Fair, and many other photography competitions. He stayed in the field for the rest of his life, working in paper-based photography and becoming a respected elder to those who followed him in the art. He is now perhaps best known for having taken some early portraits of Abraham Lincoln. But regarding this story that his image inspired Longfellow to write *Hiawatha,* we have only some possible circumstantial evidence, his own word, and nothing else. Perhaps most telling: it was only in late 1886, after every possible witness to such claims had died, that Hesler mentioned George Sumner, a daguerreotype of Minnehaha, and Henry Wadsworth Longfellow at all.[13]

THE ROCK ISLAND LINE IS THE ROAD TO RIDE

Longfellow would make the waterfall famous. Photographers following Hesler's lead showed the world what Minnehaha looked like. And at about the same time, the railroad came in to bring people by the hundreds and thousands to see the falls.

Early on, Minnesota began advertising itself to tourists, settlers, and invalids as having a perfect and health-building climate. By the early 1850s, steamboats were bringing summer visitors, especially southern slaveholders escaping the heat, to new hotels in the new territory. In February 1854, when the Chicago and Rock Island Railroad line reached across Illinois from Chicago to the Mississippi River, Minnesota was suddenly within reach of those on the East Coast as well. The accomplishment was major news, and railroad executives turned it into a national event.[14]

Railroad developers always had two overlapping goals: first, to build the railroad, and second, to sell tickets and get people onto their trains. Four months after the Chicago and Rock Island reached the river, executives built up the fanfare and public excitement by inviting as many leading newspapermen, politicians, and other executives as they could stir up to come west on a Grand Excursion: a train journey to the Mississippi, followed by a steamboat trip up the river to Minnesota Territory. Lots of their wives came along, too. No longer were people dependent on rough, slow, dirty overland travel; as George Catlin had predicted, even the ladies could manage this with ease.

The Grand Excursion was a sell-out success. The train set out from Chicago on June 5, 1854, drawn by engines festively decorated for the eight-hour journey to Rock Island, Illinois. All were celebrating the milestone: the Mississippi River had been linked to the Atlantic seaboard with iron rail. After the expected speeches—former President Millard Fillmore notably held forth—the voyage began with wavings of flags and gun salutes.[15]

On board, the guests passed the days by talking, dancing, and flirting—and always looking at the scenic and beautiful Upper Mississippi River. Cottonwoods towered over the river bottoms. Prairies flowed past in the distance, until the great limestone bluffs rose up out of the river. Galley crews served oysters and lobsters daily, having brought them along "in sealed tins," and they purchased live lambs and pigs and vegetables on shore. At least one boat had cows in the lower hold to supply fresh milk.

The steamboats arrived in St. Paul a day early, with those on shore and those on board in high excitement. The early arrival rather inconvenienced everyone. The welcoming Minnesotans scrambled to organize conveyances—they were all set for the arrival as expected the next day—as the Easterners managed their dignity with varying amounts of grace. A single horse cart allowed three crowded editors to see the sights of the Fashionable Tour; the man riding outside a coach by standing on a step, bouncing down the territorial road between St. Paul and St. Anthony Falls, holding on to the iron luggage rail atop the coach, may have been a US senator. The group toured the towns of St. Paul and St. Anthony, taking every available wagon to see the sights: St. Anthony Falls, Bde Maka Ska, Fort Snelling, and Minnehaha Falls. The guests admired the boundless, glorious country and were feted at the state capitol; by 11 PM on the day they arrived, they had returned to their steamboats and cast off for their return trip.

The entire excursion north on the river lasted about a week. But the publicity it generated was another matter. Eastern editors published glowing accounts of the Grand Excursion, which excited the public imagination for the upper river and Minnesota. Such enthusiasm may have been another route for news of Minnehaha Falls to reach Henry Wadsworth Longfellow. In fact, he may have had an in-law on the Grand Excursion. William Appleton, the son of a Massachusetts congressman of the same name, was the second cousin of Longfellow's wife, Fanny Appleton Longfellow. Among the Appletons, only this son was of the age to take the trip, and there is a report in the *New York Times* of a William Appleton listed among the prominent people on the excursion.[16]

Less than two weeks after the excursion concluded, Longfellow began to write his poem *The Song of Hiawatha.*

THE LONG ARM OF LONGFELLOW

Pretty as it is, Minnehaha Falls could not have become the destination it was without first establishing a worldwide reputation. Naughty behavior offers temporary and local notoriety, but lasting fame is bestowed by currents that are more enigmatic, more complex, more fervent.

Henry Wadsworth Longfellow was the ideal person to accomplish such a feat. If he wasn't the most important writer in 1850s America, he was certainly the country's most famous poet. The stories he told, the characters he created, and the gently persuasive moral comforts he poetically offered were a balm to a young country that was still coming into its own culturally, while also reckoning with the systemic shocks administered by the Industrial Revolution.

Henry Wadsworth Longfellow's study in his home in Cambridge, Massachusetts. *Photo by Harry Cobb Shaw, published by Bromley & Co.*

It is not surprising that his most profitable and best-selling work was *The Song of Hiawatha*. Published in 1855, the poem mythologized the Ojibwe people exactly when the violence of European-American colonization was robbing the Ojibwe of their lands—after having pushed them into conflict with Dakota and other tribes. The brutalities inflicted on Indigenous Americans were not unknown in the cities of the eastern seaboard, and industrialization was only amplifying the vertiginous rate of change for both white and Native societies. Longfellow's useful genius mythologized the Ojibwe (and this feeling extended to other Native people). By permitting his readers to revere and even mourn the Native characters in his poem, he also helped to create space for the cognitive dissonance that arose from both the white decimation of Native cultures and the industrialized destruction of the natural environment.

Longfellow was a "fireside" poet—enjoyed by families in homey settings—who wrote with emotional clarity and easy accessibility. A languages professor who traveled to Europe and a bit in New England, he never visited the Upper Mississippi River. From his home in Cambridge, Massachusetts, he was at the center of American letters, and he surrounded himself with the prominent writers, travelers, and thinkers of the day. Ideas came to him; often they stayed for dinner.

The Song of Hiawatha is an epic story of the Ojibwe people, partly based in ethnography but mostly imaginative, that largely takes place in today's Upper Peninsula of Michigan. The magical hero Hiawatha was born of Wenonah, who died anguished and deserted, killed by the "false and faithless" West Wind, who was Hiawatha's father. Hiawatha was raised by his grandmother Nokomis, "daughter of the moon," who comes to earth as a falling star. His powerful magic is apparent when he is able to outrun an arrow, crush rocks with his mittens, or stride a mile in just a step. He battles his father, going west to do it, and though he does not win, Hiawatha stops off at Minnehaha Falls on his way home to buy arrowheads from the "ancient Arrow-maker."

There he meets the Arrow-maker's daughter, "Minnehaha, Laughing Water, / Loveliest of Dacotah women," about whom he initially says nothing. Once home, he fasts for seven days, but discovers corn while fasting. He returns to Minnehaha and brings her home to marry. There's plenty more to the story, more of friends and adventures and magic, but ultimately Minnehaha dies of famine and fever in a long winter. Hiawatha mourns, then tells his people to accept the coming of the white men and himself paddles off into the sunset.[17]

While lots of this storyline is problematic—the criticisms started the week the poem was published in 1855 and have never stopped—its popularity in its day and its influence on Minnesota cannot be denied.

Longfellow names only two specific locations that one could visit today. (The Rocky Mountains, the southern shore of Lake Superior, and the Tahquamenon River, which are all mentioned in the poem, are real places, but not pin-in-the-map locales.) One is the Pipestone quarry, on Minnesota's western prairie, now designated a national monument, where Indigenous people continue to quarry the red stone used to make pipes. The other is Minnehaha Falls.

Since he never visited Minnesota, how did Longfellow come to know of Minnehaha Falls? He himself recorded some of the broader influences on his poem. For example, in 1839, Henry Rowe School-craft published an important ethnographic study of the Ojibwe people titled *Algic Researches*. Longfellow initially skimmed the work rather than studying it intently. He described it at the beginning of his writing process as "three huge quartos, ill-digested, and without any index." But it did provide legends and useful translations of some of the nouns that Longfellow included in *Hiawatha*. Though Schoolcraft got things wrong, his work preserving the Ojibwe culture was informed by his first wife. Obabaamwewe-giizhigokwe (Jane Johnston) was herself a writer and poet, educated in Ojibwe culture and language by her Ojibwe mother and in European culture by her Irish father; she is sometimes called the first Indigenous poet.[18]

Well before beginning *The Song of Hiawatha*, Longfellow had also become acquainted with George Copway (Gaagigegaabaw). He was an Ojibwe leader from Ontario, a writer, and a Methodist missionary to his people. The two met several times in the 1840s. Copway gave Longfellow a copy of his autobiography, and Longfellow helped Copway by writing letters of introduction for him on the latter's trip to Europe.

Longfellow may have seen art depicting the Minnesota landscape and Native peoples; such was not difficult to find at the time. During the 1840s and 1850s, painters crafted huge panoramas of the Mississippi River. One of these, showing the river south of St. Louis, was on display in Boston in the 1840s while Longfellow was working on his long Acadian poem, *Evangeline*. The panorama unscrolled before the audience, and Longfellow was pleased to see it. "The river comes to me instead of my going to the river; and as it is to flow through the pages of the poem, I look upon this as a special benediction." He found the scene remarkably interesting: "One seems to be sailing down the great stream, and sees the boats and the sand-banks crested with cottonwood, and the bayous by moonlight. Three miles of canvas, and a great deal of merit." Panoramas of the Upper Mississippi— north of St. Louis—also toured in New England, so Longfellow easily could have seen one of those as well.[19]

He also may have seen traveling exhibits showing scenes of the frontier and of Indigenous people. Several painters and artists went to the frontier and subsequently put together touring shows of their work. Perhaps Longfellow saw the paintings of George Catlin or John Mix Stanley. Both had shows that toured the Northeast.[20]

Seth Eastman, another respected frontier artist, was an army officer who had been in command at Fort Snelling. During two tours of duty in Minnesota, Eastman created an abundant visual record of the Native people and their villages. He also illustrated one of Schoolcraft's later works, the six-volume *Information Respecting the History, Condition and Prospects of the Indian Tribes of the United States*. Since early volumes of this set were published before Longfellow began writing *Hiawatha*, the poet may have used some of the images and information to guide his composition. He was a Harvard professor, and this work is in Harvard's libraries.[21]

Eastman's wife, Mary Henderson Eastman, had a huge, direct effect on Longfellow's poetic epic. It was Mary who attached the name "Minnehaha" to the waterfall just north of the fort. In the introduction to her 1849 book, *Dahcotah*, she describes a bit of the scenery around the fort, first noting St. Anthony Falls—the big falls—on the Mississippi. She then described "the 'Little Falls,' forty feet in height, on a stream that empties into the Mississippi. The Indians call them Mine-hah-hah or 'laughing waters.'"[22]

The Dakota words for water and curling apply to any waterfall, and contemporary evidence demonstrates that this was not their name for the falls near Bdote. Mary Eastman made the imaginative leap to "laughing water," and others jumped with her. Brown's Falls became

Minnehaha. In its July 1853 issue, *Harper's New Monthly* published a story titled "Sketches on the Upper Mississippi," featuring a woodcut engraving of the falls and stating that "in their exquisite appreciation of nature," the Native people have given this waterfall the appropriate name of "Minnihaha," or "Laughing Waters." Longfellow wrote for *Harper's* magazine, so it's safe to assume that he read it. Clearly, waves of cultural interest in the frontier and in Native people washed over the established cities of the eastern seaboard, and Longfellow was aware of these.[23]

THE HAND OF FREDRIKA BREMER

Historic bread crumbs also show a more quietly intimate connection between Longfellow and the pretty little waterfall near the Mississippi. One of the most beloved authors in America in the 1840s and 1850s enthused about the waterfall. This was a small, delicate, calm woman from Sweden named Fredrika Bremer.

The American public adored Miss Bremer, whose works, like Longfellow's, reflected everyday realities. Newsboys hawked her novels to eager passengers at railroad stops. Walt Whitman said her stories were unusually interesting and charming and infused the reader with "a sun-lit warmth" of gentle moral instruction; after the New Testament, he recommended that every family own Miss Bremer's works. Bremer was a decided abolitionist, a stance that would have extended her appeal among the New England elites in antebellum America.[24]

As a novelist, Bremer was a reformer and a social critic. Even as her writing expressed her pleasing, sweet personality, it promoted women's rights and women's education. People loved her.

In 1849, with her family back home unsettled by her choice to travel alone, Bremer left Sweden to visit America. She felt "magnetized by the western world" and wanted to see firsthand how the New World treated women, to see their homes, and to understand the happiness of the people under their democratic government. (She read Longfellow's *Evangeline* during the Atlantic crossing; she thought the ending—where Evangeline finally reunites with her long-lost love on his deathbed—was melodramatic and somewhat labored.)[25]

One of her American correspondents was Andrew Jackson Downing, a notable New York horticulturist. Downing helped her with introductions to his broad social network. In December 1849, Bremer traveled to Cambridge, Massachusetts, where she stayed at the home of Maria and James Russell Lowell and was welcomed by the town's writers, abolitionists, social reformers, and poets. This group naturally included Henry Wadsworth Longfellow.[26]

Longfellow was clearly fond of her. He said she was a kindly old lady. (Fanny Longfellow said she was "the soul of gentleness—a most loveable old maid." Bremer was forty-eight, just seven years older than Henry.) He noted that she had gentle manners, a soft voice, and a lovely face that reminded him of John Keats; paintings of both show he was right. At their first meeting, they talked of Swedish authors, some of whom were well known to Longfellow. He must have enjoyed the visit. He and Fanny saw her two more times that December, and they had her to dinner on December 20, 1849.[27]

A dozen authors, actors, translators, and even Longfellow's great friend Senator Charles Sumner gathered around the table in the poet's dining room for canvasback ducks and quail. The Longfellows served Roman punch, a fancy drink made from orange juice, lemonade, rum, champagne, and plenty of sugar, poured over ice and topped with meringue. Its presence on the menu shows how important this party was to the hosts. They also served three kinds of American wine: Scuppernong, Gabella, and Cincinnati's famous Sparkling Catawba. Longfellow thought the party was something of a triumph—he described the evening as "very charming"—and Fanny was pleased, too. Bremer thought it very excellent, with very good wines and fine guests. She called Longfellow an agreeable host.[28]

Bremer and Longfellow crossed paths in Cambridge during subsequent visits and dinners in January and February of 1850. After one event, he complimented her, saying she had been "the lioness, though all modesty and humility." His interest in her is unmistakable, and she treated his interest kindly. She began a sketch of him in her journal, and she agreed to accompany him to have a plaster cast of her right hand made for Fanny, who remarked on many occasions about how small Bremer's hands were. On that morning, Longfellow "could not sit still, but must needs go to town." The plaster cast had to be postponed, so he squired her around Boston on a tiring long walk. Miss Bremer—a notable introvert—found the outing exhausting enough to be seen by a doctor the next day. Nevertheless, they spent that second long day together and finally had the plaster cast made. Of the attention, Bremer only said that it was "a prevailing error that [her] hands were beautiful, whereas they are only delicate and small."[29]

These insistent and even manufactured reasons—a trait he'd also shown while courting Fanny—whereby Longfellow spent time with Bremer leave little room for doubt: he was truly fond of her.

Bremer eventually left the comforts and attention of Cambridge society and headed west to tour America, making the trip to the Minnesota Territory in the autumn of 1850. She traveled by steamers, trains, and stagecoaches across the Great Lakes, Michigan, and Wisconsin, eventually boarding the steamboat *Nominee* in Galena for the trip to St. Paul. On the same boat were Territorial Representative Henry Hastings Sibley and his wife, who were returning home from Washington. Miss Bremer wrote of Sibley, "Sometimes when we sail past Indian villages, he utters a kind of wild cry which receives an exulting response from the shore." At this time, the Dakota held the western shore of the Mississippi, and white settlement was not permitted there. Territorial Governor Alexander Ramsey himself took Bremer to Fort Snelling so that she could observe and meet the Native people camped there. Along the way, they stopped off at Minnehaha Falls. As she described it, "We visited, on our way to Fort Snelling, a waterfall, called the Little Falls. It is small, but so infinitely beautiful that it deserves its own picture, song, and saga. The whitest of foam, the blackest of crags, the most graceful, and at the same time wild and gentle fall! Small things may become great through their perfection."[30]

Longfellow had those words in his hands in October 1853, when Bremer's *The Homes of the New World: Impressions of America* was published. He acquired a copy the week it went on sale, and unlike Copway's autobiography, Fredrika Bremer's work is still in Longfellow's library. Perhaps this passage planted a seed in the poet's heart. Perhaps he wished to connect himself and Bremer through this beautiful place. He, too, concluded that Minnehaha Falls deserved its own saga. After all, as a poet, sagas were a specialty of his.

The Song of Hiawatha was a remarkable success, going into a second printing the week it was published. The London newspapers reviewed it, argued over it, and elevated it. In less than two years, *Hiawatha* sold over fifty thousand copies. It was known all over the world and translated into many languages. And with that success came the curious and reverential, who, like Hiawatha in the poem, journeyed

> Till he heard the cataract's laughter,
> Heard the Falls of Minnehaha
> Calling to him through the silence.
> "Pleasant is the sound!" he murmured,
> "Pleasant is the voice that calls me!"

And when these curious, reverential travelers arrived at Minnehaha, the locally and world-famous waterfall, they found on a largely empty prairie an ever-increasing scene of hospitality.

3

Monetizing the Falls

MINNEHAHA HAD BECOME, and would continue to be, a famous destination. It made good sense to provide for visitors who were drawn to the waterfall. They wanted refreshments and meals, souvenirs, and even a place to stay. For the next thirty years, the available hospitality at Minnehaha would become increasingly elaborate, and eventually just too undeniably liquored up. The early landowners, catering to the soldiers, townspeople, and all those tourists, set it in motion.

HOW IT BEGAN

The actions of two settler families directly and indirectly caused Minnehaha, the revered and beloved Minnehaha, to be turned into what the *Minneapolis Journal* would call "a place of reproach and shame." The first was Franklin Steele and his family, who were important landowners in the area from Minnesota's early days. Steele specifically saw Minnehaha as a place that could help increase his wealth. The second was territorial pioneer George W. Lincoln and his family, who were in business with Steele and helped maintain and enlarge Steele's business interests at the falls. Of the two patriarchs, Steele was the richer and older man.[1]

Land ownership at the falls is a wildly complicated mess of sales and resales, fractional ownership, foreclosures, lawsuits, and inheritances, so tracing the exact owner of any given square yard of ground is an immense task. But the outlines of the story are clear enough. Franklin Steele, the fort sutler and the man who managed to claim that invaluable land on the Mississippi at the Falls of St. Anthony in

1839, was particularly focused on Minnehaha Falls and its environs. He bought some of the ground around Minnehaha Falls twice or even three times. Yet he seems not to have left any explanation for his attachment to the falls. While he may have loved the beauty of the falling waters, his actions were all about making money from the place.[2]

On August 26, 1852, Congress again redefined the boundaries of the military reservation. This time, it was to be bounded by the Mississippi River to the east and the Minnesota to the south. To the west, it ended about where Cedar Avenue runs today, and Minnehaha Creek was the boundary to the north. Claimants took possession of the land on the creek's north bank. And even before Congress passed this act, Patrick Maloney had constructed his claim cabin on the north side of Minnehaha Falls. Maloney was there to challenge and greet Alexander Hesler and Joel Whitney when they arrived to take the first photograph of Minnehaha Falls. Ard Godfrey, the man Steele had hired to construct the mill at St. Anthony Falls, took a claim of 147 acres where Minnehaha Creek emptied into the river.[3]

Both those claims were legally purchased in 1855, and Godfrey would stay on his parcel for decades. How Steele acquired ownership of Maloney's claim is not clear. At least from 1851, one Patrick Maloney owed Steele's sutler store various amounts of money, at one point over a hundred dollars. Some dispute caused these men to sue each other, and Steele ultimately lost, though he had a lien on the judgment. Whatever the transactional details, ultimately Steele acquired this land and began to monetize it.[4]

Steele's Little Falls Farm on the Maloney claim at Minnehaha Falls was a going concern in the 1850s. Sometime around 1867, Franklin and Annie Steele built an expansive house there for their large family. Much later, Steele's children inherited a house on that same parcel of land, which suggests that it is the same structure. The house stood at the intersection of Minnehaha Avenue, East Minnehaha Parkway, and Godfrey Parkway. There's a traffic circle there today. He used the farm to grow wheat and oats and potatoes, but he also provided hospitality at the falls.[5]

Steele expanded his landholdings from the Maloney claim to a much, much bigger piece of land. In 1857, and once again using eastern capital and his political connections, he made his most dubious land purchase, buying Fort Snelling and the military reservation—lock,

Minnehaha in early spring, about 1859. Some of the first buildings on Franklin Steele's Little Falls Farm are visible in the distance. *Photo by Benjamin Franklin Upton*

stock, and barrel. Henry M. Rice, the territorial delegate from Minnesota, was in Washington and heard news of the reservation's upcoming sale, then alerted Steele. Steele partnered with speculators from New York and Virginia, who gave him a full one-third interest. Commissioners (including the officer-artist Seth Eastman) were appointed to broker the transaction, and one of Steele's partners accompanied the group of commissioners traveling from Washington to Minnesota. Perhaps influenced by this partner, the commissioners decided to sell the entire reservation as a single parcel (only big-money players would have a chance at it), and they wrote to Steele asking for his bid. For $30,000 and the promise of two later payments of the same size, the entire fort was turned over to Steele and his partners in 1858. No other bids were entertained. Locals protested vehemently, but after a congressional investigation into this shady deal, the sale was allowed.[6]

The military left Fort Snelling, but then returned in April of 1861, when the government commandeered the fort, using it to muster troops for the Civil War. Finally, in 1868, and after more congressional hearings into the highly questionable, shady nature of the purchase, the ownership of the military reservation and the fort was settled. The government paid Steele for renting his fort during the war, and Steele had them subtract from that amount the two final payments he had never made and had no plans to volunteer—he was waiting to be asked to pay up. The government kept about 1,500 acres, including the area at the confluence of the rivers and the old fort buildings, while Steele and partners retained the other 6,400 acres across today's Minneapolis and Richfield. It cost them about nine dollars per acre. Again, locals howled, asserting the land was worth fifty dollars per acre.

During his ownership, Steele considered turning the fort's acreage into the city of Fort Snelling—the plan failed—but he found other ways to make the most of the growing fame of Minnehaha Falls. After twenty years as the sutler at the fort, he knew people. He sold the Baker claim to Kenneth McKenzie on September 1, 1857. (McKenzie was leasing the St. Louis Hotel already; now he owned the land underneath it. By 1859, he sold the Baker claim to someone from St. Louis named Adam Stewart.)[7]

Steele had an established trading network. He was skilled at moving goods and was well known to the soldiers and settlers in the area. The Grand Excursion and Henry Wadsworth Longfellow had placed a spotlight on Minnesota and Minnehaha Falls, and thanks to the army's whiskey rations, Joe Brown, and Kenneth McKenzie, the area was firmly connected with drink. Steele knew that the combination of the famous Minnehaha Falls and drink was an irresistible invitation. From at least 1859, and probably from his ownership of the military reservation, Steele built and owned a "rural refreshment house" at Minnehaha Falls.[8]

This roadhouse became the Minnehaha Hotel, a small precursor to the larger and grander hotel that would dominate the south side of the falls in the early 1880s. It was built on the south side of the creek, along the edge of the gorge, and close to the waterfall. At the restaurant, "homemade dinners can be had for seventy-five cents a head. There is no charge of any kind to visit the falls, and the place is much frequented by picnic parties." Early on, the place was under the care of someone named Boyden—possibly Augustus, maybe George— who was known to have run "first class accommodations there in 1863–4." At this time, the place began to be called the Minnehaha Hotel, though we don't know how many rooms it had, or who stayed there, or other details.[9]

During the Civil War, the government had no military use for the far reaches of the reservation where the Minnehaha Hotel was located, but hard-drinking soldiers surely found the bar an attractive destination. Regardless, the character and reputation of the place were called "strictly first class." Boyden might have taken the position

The first Minnehaha Hotel, about 1863. *Photo by E. & H. T. Anthony*

because he expected the railroad to come through and bring him carloads of delighted tourists. But that wouldn't happen until 1865, after the war's end.[10]

The Steeles left Minnesota and moved to Washington, DC, in 1867. Perhaps the new railroad, which ran just outside their door, had become an unbearable annoyance. But perhaps it is not a coincidence that they left the area at the same time that, as the paper reported it, "hundreds of people were daily visiting this charming spot."[11]

The hardworking George Lincoln

Though Steele owned many thousands of acres of open land in what is today the city of Minneapolis, he wasn't a farmer in the sense that he ever stood at one end of the plow himself. He hired people for that. And one of the people who worked with him most was George W. Lincoln.

Like Ard Godfrey and many other of Minnesota's territorial settlers, George Lincoln came from Maine. A generation younger than Steele—he was twenty-two in 1857—he initially lived in a boardinghouse in St. Anthony and made his living as a teamster. By the 1860s, however, he was living on the military reservation and running the ferry that Steele operated from the fort across the Mississippi River. He became a trusted partner to Steele, collecting tolls and turning over the money. Lincoln became a landowner and definitely was involved in other businesses with Steele, including supplying the army with beef and other rations during the Civil War.[12]

George's wife, Vinette Southard (or Southworth), had come to Minnesota from Maine in 1863. Before long, they had three daughters. In 1866, George and Vinette established a homestead on the north side of Coldwater Spring, where he farmed 150 acres of the former military reservation. Four years later, quite a number of people were living with them there, including some farmworkers, other boarders, and an Englishman named Thomas Wallgate.

Early in 1871, the Lincoln house burned to the ground. It was a horrendous nighttime blaze, bright enough to cast shadows miles away on the dark streets of Minneapolis. Wallgate and two others were home when the fire began, and though they heroically (and foolishly) went back into the burning building to save what they could,

The ferry across the Mississippi from Fort Snelling, about 1875. *Published by William Illingsworth*

nearly everything was lost. All the furniture inside was uninsured. Lincoln was out of state at the time, and Vinette and the little girls may have been with him. When he returned to Minneapolis the next day, there was literally no home to return to.[13]

George had been business partners with Wallgate, importing breeding stock for racehorses from England. Unsurprisingly, the partnership ended at the time of the fire, though Lincoln's interest in horse racing—a popular activity in Minnesota at the time—shows he was increasingly becoming a man of means.

After the fire, the Lincolns moved into the large house just northwest of Minnehaha Falls that had been the home of Franklin and Annie Steele.

Lincoln's partnership with Steele grew over the next few decades, and every step they took was in pursuit of financial prosperity. Though Steele had moved with his family to Washington, he returned frequently to Minnesota. He even kept rooms at a St. Paul hotel for

The Steele-Lincoln house in the early 1900s, after it had been moved to
5028 Hiawatha Avenue. The house still stands. *HCL*

a time. But beginning in the late 1860s, the main person keeping an
eye on their business concerns at Minnehaha was George Lincoln.

DOES ANYBODY KNOW HOW TO RUN
A HOTEL AND RESTAURANT?

After the Civil War, Captain Milo Palmer was put in charge of running the rural refreshment house, the earliest version of the Minnehaha Hotel. Palmer, a Civil War veteran, had served with the Twelfth
Wisconsin Infantry and was injured at Vicksburg (the paralysis in
his left leg was "severe but not total"). After his injury, he was ordered to Fort Snelling, which he commanded until the war's end. He
was mustered out in June 1866. About a year later, his pension came
through, and two months after that, he was managing the refreshment house. It was a festive place. Palmer even found a way to illuminate the waterfall at night by using calcium lights. This technology,
also called limelight, was used to light up theater stages for evening
performances in this same era. The illuminated waterfall was a show-
stopping occurrence in a place that didn't yet have electric lights.[14]

Palmer offered ice cream and lemonade but also choice wines and liquors. And he was prepared to serve meals and drinks at any time, so late-night carousers were welcomed there. It was a year-around establishment. In November of 1869, just as the waterfall was beginning to freeze, St. Paul photographer Charles Zimmerman came to Minnehaha, probably to photograph the waterfall. As he went clambering around behind the fall, a huge icicle came loose, fell on him, and knocked him out. When he was found by chance thirty minutes later, he was carried to Palmer's place, where "the proper restoratives were administered." Surely, that meant whiskey.[15]

Even after losing his home in the 1871 fire, Lincoln still had the wherewithal to acquire the creek's south bank at the falls by buying hundreds of acres of the old military reservation from Steele's partners in the fort purchase. Minnehaha Avenue was platted, running from the growing city of Minneapolis through the country farms straight to the famous waterfall. Since 1865, the railroad had connected Minneapolis to the big eastern cities (and offered locals cheap round-trip fares to and from Minneapolis), and now the new road was going in. Getting to Minnehaha had never been easier, and Lincoln decided to make improvements on the hotel.

He spent $30,000 on the project. He enlarged the barroom and kitchen, built a new bar, and improved the dining room. Parlors were refurnished, plans were developed for a huge barn for stabling guests' horses and rigs, and a newsstand went up that sold fruit and candy and had a sitting room just for the ladies. Picnic parties were invited to use the newly built picnic tables and provided with free ice. Because dancing was a primary way that men and women socialized, Lincoln also had a large outdoor dancing platform built on the grounds. Lincoln improved another one of Palmer's amenities as well. Palmer's son Albert had taken photos at the falls for a few years—he had a bad tendency to overexpose his pictures—but Lincoln built a brand-new photography gallery on the south side of the Minnehaha gorge so that visitors could have their picture taken right in front of the falls. Milo Palmer then seems to have moved his hospitality north to a house known as the Adams House. Boyden, who had been invited back to manage the house at Minnehaha, advertised "Meals with all the luxuries of the season, at all hours, and any quantity of ice cream."[16]

Newspaper stories excitingly reported all of these improvements, but they also warned Lincoln and Steele, "the falls are unsurpassed in the world in point of fairy-like beauty, and nature has set upon the surroundings the seal of earthly perfection. It now remains for the proprietors to treat with courtesy and consideration all tourists and visitors, and keep the house and grounds free from rowdyism." The mention of rowdyism shows that it was already a known occurrence at Minnehaha.[17]

Boyden stayed on as manager for just a year, and the property was next leased to Colonel John J. Shaw from St. Paul. Shaw was a highly experienced and successful hotel man. Having built the Merchants Hotel in St. Paul into a large and profitable business, he leased that to someone else. He moved to Minnehaha, took out a six-year lease at $3,000 per year, and set out to add onto the hotel at the falls. It was August of 1873, and he expected to invest $50,000 in the project. A visitor from New York snidely wondered if the new proprietors would serve cooked chicken.[18]

The timing was ideal for this next leap in the development and growth taking place at Minnehaha Falls. After a wildly complex era on the military reservation, with years of continuing sales and resales, collaborations and collusions, congressional investigations, a couple of wars, and the seemingly endless redrawing of the old military reservation's boundaries, an auction was held in 1873 to dispose of much of the remaining government land. Lincoln and Steele finally gained ownership of Minnehaha Falls, and Shaw leased the property immediately after that.[19]

Shaw planned to improve the existing building. It had been almost sixty-five years since the Fifth Infantry had first arrived at the confluence of the rivers. Back then, they beat the winter weather as they constructed their shelter, though only barely. Shaw took possession of the lease in August, but he had the luxury of a growing modern city a few miles away that he could retreat to during the winter. He also had rail transportation, and he knew that Minnehaha Avenue, a new road to the falls, would be opening soon. He was in no hurry to begin the work.

Also, he didn't have a liquor license. During the 1874 season, Shaw applied for a license from the town of Richfield, which acquired jurisdiction over the area after the military reservation was pulled back, but the application was rejected: the town had voted not to allow liquor sales. Palmer, who was now running a restaurant in the Adams House just north on Minnehaha Avenue, had been told the same thing. Happily for all their patrons who were looking for a drink, a technicality intervened. Someone pointed out that the Richfield board had not published the proceedings of their meeting, and somehow this technicality invalidated their dry vote.[20]

Shaw should have been in good shape to succeed at Minnehaha. The location couldn't be beat. He had the skills, and he now had his liquor license. His cocktails were superlative. And yet, much appears to have gone badly wrong. In September of 1874, his lease wasn't paid, his chattel mortgage was foreclosed on, and the hotel closed.[21]

George Lincoln, who was seemingly never afraid of work, turned to the job of completing the upgrade of the hotel. Planning for thirty guest rooms and a new stable, he thought the work would take just two weeks, a remarkably ambitious timeline. The newly enlarged hotel and the path to its doorway were perfectly aligned opposite the depot on the Milwaukee Road, which had been built in 1875. (Still standing, the depot is the oldest structure in the park and has long been called the Little Princess for its petite and charming affect.) The setting was ideally welcoming.[22]

Thomas W. Hanson, who became manager of the new hotel in 1875, was known as a jovial host who offered "noticeable perfection" as well as a free lunch at the turkey shoots he occasionally hosted on the grounds. He stayed on through the winter of 1875–76. A leap year began, and apparently a Sadie Hawkins tradition—though it wasn't known by that name—was observed at the time. On several evenings that winter, a sleigh full of young ladies drove around town to pick up some beaux, then drove out to the Minnehaha Hotel, where the girls asked the young men to dance. It was all innocent fun, but everyone knew it was not the regular order of society. The young ladies further pranked their fellows by hiding the key to the bar. Hanson also illuminated the falls and even put on fireworks shows, but ultimately he faded into Minnehaha's history and left only a bit of advertising behind.[23]

In 1876 and 1877 and into 1878, the lease passed from one person to another. With every change of management, newspapers dropped hints that unseemly activities were available at the falls. Why else would there be the recurring expectations that "things were being greatly improved"?[24]

The issue that always lurked in the background and that defined activity at Minnehaha was the sale of property. And as the land was split and sold and then resold again, Isadore Henry came to own a few acres just south of the Minnehaha Hotel.

Henry was a German-speaking immigrant, probably from Alsace, and thus he was known as Dutch Henry by his many, many friends. He came to Minnesota in 1871 and opened bathing rooms in the United States Hotel on Bridge Square in downtown Minneapolis; both hot and cold baths were on offer. That sounded useful and respectable enough at a time when many people did not have indoor plumbing, but within months, Henry had moved on to running a saloon. In these early days, he took out a liquor license for this establishment. He wouldn't always bother to do so. Dutch Henry was tough. Once, when his landlord complained about the fiddle music in the dance hall, Henry grabbed him by the throat and threw him out of the building.[25]

Assaulting his landlord likely cost him the saloon and sent him a few miles south, to set up his new hotel and dance hall at Minnehaha. Like Steele and Lincoln, he planned to make money from the crowds who visited the falls. He called his place, at the west end of the current Soldiers' Home bridge along Minnehaha Avenue, the Minnehaha Spring Garden Hotel, but most people just called it Henry's Place. Even after the move, Henry continued to be a tough character; he was once found guilty of assaulting his bartender for making incorrect change.

In 1875, a comic performance troupe named the Adelphi Comedy and Burlesque Company caused a stir when they traveled to Minneapolis from Chicago and set up a permanent show in a downtown theater. They advertised *legerdemain* and "comicalities"—this coded word was often used for performances mocking African Americans—and said that ladies and children were welcome. But when they played at Henry's establishment, the show was called an indecent and disgraceful exhibition designed for an audience of "roughs and rowdies." (Perhaps women showed their limbs as well.) Newspapers, ever the arbiters of public acceptability, said that decent people would be forced to avoid the falls if such shows were allowed to continue. But even with such reprimands, or perhaps because of them, the Adelphi Sunday performances at Minnehaha drew large crowds.[26]

And indeed, an anonymous letter defending the falls from attacks on decency was published soon after this. In strong terms, it stated that Mr. George Lincoln had nothing to do with the rowdyism, carryings-on, and disturbances that were occurring at another property near the falls. The letter writer had "a deep interest in maintaining intact [the falls'] reputation for peace and quiet." The tone was so thoroughly supportive of the Minnehaha Hotel and Lincoln that it's quite possible it was written by his wife, Vinette. If so, it's an early revelation of her protective nature. Vinette Lincoln would eventually prove herself to be a powerful, litigious force in the story of Minnehaha Park and the hospitality offered there.[27]

The mayhem continued. Fort Snelling had become the headquarters for the US Army's Department of Dakota; soldiers moved through the post on their way to billets in the West. Henry catered to the soldiers from the fort, as they were the perfect clientele: hard-drinking, close at hand, and with money to spend. He hired the Fort Snelling Band to play at dances at his place and advertised to attract ladies. His dance hall became known for "promiscuous gatherings of men and women of loose morals." He ignored the ban on Sunday liquor sales, a decision that led to reports of robberies and stabbings among his patrons. This was a rough spot, and rowdy behavior of one sort or another was not out of the ordinary. Soldiers went to Henry's Place to drink before, say, heading out to rob citizens, as happened to a farmer from Mendota in 1878. Men from town went out to fight with the soldiers over who should be "allowed" to drink there. The military police from the fort were sometimes called in to keep order.[28]

In 1879, Henry came up with a plan to reach even more customers by putting on minstrel shows. Maybe he wanted to redeem his establishment and invite a somewhat "better" class of people. Maybe he liked the returns from the Adelphi shows and wanted to try again. This was an era when America's chief entertainments included drinking, dancing, and racial hatred. This loathing was taught to white Americans through jokes and songs still sung today: "Oh! Susanna," "Hard Times," "Camptown Races," and dozens of other songs from the era were all originally written to be performed in minstrel shows.

From the 1840s and into the twentieth century, minstrel troupes, of ever-increasing size and outlandishness, traveled all over America. White people used shoe polish or burnt cork to darken their skin and perform demeaning caricatures of Black people; vicious stereotypes that came from minstrelsy still poison American perceptions of its own racist past. Because Dutch Henry's hall was not as big as some of the performance halls downtown, the traveling shows didn't play there. Instead, Henry assembled his own group. With the help of a downtown saloon-runner named Johnson, a profoundly unsavory person, he hired local entertainers to perform minstrel shows at the falls. The troupe played both Johnson's saloon and Henry's Place, and "hundreds of visitors every week" saw the show. It could not have been an especially impressive performance—one act was a harmonica solo—and the performances did not continue through the season. It could be that the undisciplined crowds who frequented Henry's Place grew tired of the show and that more refined folks wouldn't consider attending.[29]

Henry's partnership with Johnson didn't turn out to be as lucrative as he'd planned, so he continued to boost his income with alcohol sales. Not having a license didn't stop him, and neither did the courts. In 1879, he was charged with selling liquor and beer without a license and with selling to minors. The fines were seventy-five dollars each, but to Henry, this was (and would continue to be) the cost of doing business.[30]

These activities were all taking place in the far reaches of the county; the growing city was a long way away, and so were the moral strictures of the Yankee work ethic. The era of sentimentality over Longfellow's poem was washing away, and at Minnehaha was being replaced by boozy chaos. But Minnehaha Falls was still picturesque, still beloved, and the Lincolns were still trying to keep a better class of people coming to visit.

What Minnehaha needs is a florist

John Booth, an Englishman, arrived in Minneapolis in 1871, the same year as Dutch Henry. A florist and grower who had brought his trade with him from England, Booth worked with the early Minneapolis nurseryman Wyman Elliott at an establishment at Tenth and Chicago Avenue and then eventually bought three acres east of the depot at Minnehaha for a new landscape business.[31]

George Lincoln sold him this land, situated as a buffer between

Lincoln's Minnehaha Hotel to the north and Henry's Minnehaha Spring Garden Hotel to the south. In April of 1873, he was already well established in Minnehaha, having built a greenhouse "and bountifully stocked it with rare and beautiful plants." He helped George Lincoln and John Shaw beautify the grounds around their hotel, and by 1877, he had built himself a house and moved his entire operation to Minnehaha.[32]

At first, Booth was primarily a grower. He stocked bedding plants that he sold locally and by train as far away as Fargo, North Dakota. Conveniently, the train stopped at the depot just across Minnehaha Avenue from Booth's Gardens. For those in need of a bouquet or wreath, it was the work of a moment for him to put one together.

Booth and his staff worked hard to create a showplace garden on his grounds. His plan was to cater to visitors at the falls, and viewing Booth's gardens was always free. He believed flowers should be affordable to every family. He built several light summer houses with thatched roofs and twining vines that were surrounded with "unlimited flowers." He intended to welcome visitors to a beautiful, shaded spot to rest and enjoy cool drinks within the sound of the falls. He offered picnic supplies, souvenirs like "Indian curiosities," stereoview pictures and mementos of Minnehaha Falls, and of course, "all kinds of refreshments."[33]

African American gardeners working in John Booth's flower beds, about 1881.
Photo by Michael Nowack

Soon enough, Booth's Gardens was a popular stop for people making the visit to the falls. And to add to the interest and excitement, Booth acquired—somehow, though the details are lost to history—a live alligator, which he kept in an iron cage and very likely fed in some public and thrilling fashion.[34]

SOMEBODY? ANYBODY? WHO WANTS TO RUN A HOTEL?

Finding someone to run the Minnehaha Hotel remained a challenge. The responsibility for managing the hotel landed in 1878 with John Hall. Hall hailed from Iowa and was looking to improve his fortunes. He hoped, if he were successful, to purchase some land at Minnehaha. He intended to redeem the place from whatever unwritten but unsavory hijinks happened there. "The first step he will take to bringing the place into good repute," reported the *Tribune*, "will be to close the bar."[35]

That same summer, the public began to enjoy the idea of making a day at the falls by visiting Booth's Gardens after having dinner at the hotel. For others, champagne and oysters in the wee hours of the morning comprised a popular night out. Whatever good repute was said to be lacking might have been due to the rowdy spillover from Henry's Place to the south or the certainty that some of those oyster and champagne indulgers should have been home in bed with their spouses. The newspaper alluded to some ill-defined but pleasurable activity by saying "a walk to Minnehaha and back before breakfast is getting to be the most popular constitutional among our young men." Whatever that meant—and it certainly wasn't about young men going to view the pretty little waterfall in the early morning—it was a sign that things at Minnehaha were perhaps livelier than most people knew. And the situation was about to become even more exciting.[36]

John Hall wasn't the one who made the change, however. Due to failing health, he was unable to accomplish anything substantial at the Minnehaha Hotel. Exactly one month after he took the lease, and probably before he had time to close the bar as promised, he sold out to Hugh Donnelly from St. Paul.

Donnelly seemed perfectly suited for the job, bringing energy and excitement to the hotel's operations. With Donnelly at the helm, said the *St. Paul Globe,* the place had "none of the objectionable features which characterize many places of public resort." He was genial and agreeable, and he was "ever alert and steadfast in his efforts to please." This description, of course, is all lightly coded language that was intended to reassure the moral, better-off class of people that a visit to the falls would not be marred by staggering drunk men and women with loose corset ties.[37]

There's no question that Donnelly was an able host. He held concerts by the top bands of the day and was able to serve two hundred people for dinner on just a couple hours' notice. His advertisements, with enticing and genteel mentions of ices and refreshments served in the grounds' pavilions, promised that "You cannot pass the day more agreeably" and "Everything will be done to insure comfort and enjoyment." That surely would have been attractive to the ladies.[38]

And yet. In order to have a successful business, Donnelly needed crowds, and those crowds wanted alcohol, which he would cheerfully supply: "Gentlemen who understand their business were running the Minnehaha Hotel," the *Globe* observed. It was now "the 'boss' place for a pleasure resort." Donnelly was noted for his ability to "minister to the inner man," an altogether odd way of saying that he provided food and drink and fun. By October, nothing was being said about Donnelly's ways, but boisterous and rowdy drunks were getting arrested on trains leaving the falls. Unlike his predecessors, Donnelly decided to run a seasonal operation, so he shut down for the winter and reopened on May 1, 1879. All was to be, as we have heard before, "strictly first class."[39]

The competition at the falls intensified. Isadore Henry offered Sunday entertainment in mid-April: "Song and dance, seriocomic vocalists, and the inimitable Barney the musical moke." (A "musical moke" was a blackface musician who performed on multiple instruments; "moke" was both a term for a donkey and a racist term.) Within weeks, Henry was back in court on liquor violations, paying seventy-five dollars for each infraction and another four hundred dollars in bail. Donnelly was also selling illegal alcohol, but perhaps because his operation was just a bit more respectable, he was a little less of a target and received preferential treatment from the courts. By the end of May, he had been charged, convicted, and fined a total of forty dollars. Printed beside the story of his conviction and fine was a pronouncement stating that "Minnehaha never appeared at

DONNELLY'S

Minnehaha Hotel

Is located immediately at the Falls, and has connected with it the entire grounds about the beautiful waterfall.

It is kept in a STRICTLY FIRST-CLASS manner, and guests are accommodated on either the American or European plan.

Regular Rate, $3.00 per Day.

The Table d'Hote and the Parlor Restaurant

will be found supplied with the very best of everything in the market, excellently prepared and served.

Ices and Light Refreshments

are served to order in the prettily furnished parlors or in the pavilions, and a Lunch Counter will supply the needs of excursion parties.

THE FAMOUS GREAT WESTERN BAND

Will give occasional concerts on the premises.

Hugh Donnelly's brochure for the Minnehaha Hotel, about 1879

better advantage until now . . . the myriads of wild flowers, ferns, and moss clothe the soil in glorious color." Donnelly's hotel was refitted and ready for the season's crowds, and there was "no place in the state where people who love nature and order can better spend the day than at Minnehaha."[40]

Donnelly's reputation remained intact. Families enjoyed the falls through the summer of 1879, and it seemed Minnehaha was "just regaining its old enviable reputation." He hired the premier musical outfit of the day, the Great Western Band, to play a series of Sunday concerts. All seemed morally and socially acceptable. So why, at the height of summer, did the *Tribune* print that Donnelly "sure knows how to make friends"? The respectable people did not go to the falls to make friends. The rounders at his bar surely did.[41]

New Englanders like George Lincoln and Ard Godfrey and the leaders of Minneapolis had brought west with them blue laws, which restricted Sunday sales and activities like dancing, shows, entertainments, shopping, and sports. For the most part, such laws were unenforceable and unenforced. Both Donnelly and Henry catered to the people who did not care about such things and who simply wanted to relax and enjoy their visit to Minnehaha, pretty often with a drink or two.

This was very much a class issue. People of means enjoyed attending church and otherwise spent Sundays quietly at home. For these folks, such activities were a fitting observation of the Lord's Day, and they were concerned about the community's growing tendency to disregard the Sabbath. In 1879, a few local businessmen called a meeting, reported in the *Minneapolis Tribune*, to discuss the problem that led to the pernicious fun and lack of moral restraint that was occurring at the falls. The newspaper reporter went to the office of Joseph Dean (one of the first three Hennepin County commissioners, a banker and businessman; the city named Dean Parkway for him). Dean had called the meeting but later denied it ever took place. He then laid out the problem as he saw it. Property and business interests required the moral restraint of resting on Sunday, and the city's inhabitants would be improved by "regarding" the day. David C. Bell (a mortgage lender whose name is still found on Bell Bank) added to the story: "Observance of the Sabbath has been growing more and more lax for several years past." He lamented that pleasure was the first dangerous attack on the Sabbath, and said that "going with his family to church and passing the rest of the Sabbath quietly at home would be more refreshing to any man than a day of out-door pleasure at Minnehaha or other resort to say nothing of the dissipation which such modes of spending the Sabbath inevitably lead to." He believed that if Sunday were a day of pleasure it would become a day of labor for others, so that working men ought to rigidly preserve the Sabbath as a matter of self-interest. These moralistic, clean-living businessmen were on a purity crusade against the working class. They thought that moral pressure was more likely to change the minds of the working class than trying to enforce the Sunday laws. At the time, the law read: "No person shall keep open a shop, warehouse or workhouse, or shall do any manner of labor, business or work, except only works of necessity and charity or be present at any dancing, or any public diversion, show or entertainment, or take part in any sport, game or play on the Lord's day, commonly called Sunday; and every person so offending shall be punished by a fine not exceeding two dollars."[42]

Attendees thought that the moral certitude that came with this argument would be more persuasive than any attempt to enforce the blue laws. That didn't work. But the meeting's pious, moralizing outcome defined again the two sides of an argument that would continue at Minnehaha. The class lines separating people became increasingly clear, and the wealthier folks felt free to opine about the actions of the working class. Before long, they felt even more free to force their will upon them as well.

Donnelly continued to walk the tightrope, trying to cater to both edges of this class struggle. He maintained a fine dining room, yet offered band concerts on Sunday. He may have managed to continue his balancing act—he was good at it—but fate intervened when his brother died suddenly, leaving behind a widow, a child, and a saloon on Wabasha Street in St. Paul. Donnelly moved back across the river to take care of it all. When he went looking to sell the lease on his hotel business, he quickly found a competent man right at hand. This is when John Booth, the horticulturalist, stepped up and took over the Minnehaha Hotel.[43]

JOHN BOOTH AND THE MINNEHAHA HOTEL

Booth began his tenure as the hotel's manager in February of 1880 by hosting a party to celebrate the new venture. He had observed the hotel's clientele and operations for about seven years, and he understood the kinds of people who frequented the falls. From his own refreshment pavilion experience, he seems to have understood the

Minnehaha Hotel, about 1881. *Published by Union View Company*

line between proper society and the tippling class, and like Donnelly, he catered to both. John Booth did get arrested for illegal alcohol sales, but he also had very light fines to pay. Booth also had a bit less reverence for the belovedness of Minnehaha Falls than Donnelly. It was Booth who had an alligator on his premises, after all. He is the one who put in hurdy-gurdy swings and a small roller coaster. (Alas, no picture seems to exist of the entertainments he provided.)[44]

Within days of Booth's taking over the Minnehaha Hotel, Minneapolis's mayor Alonzo Cooper Rand received a petition concerning the Sunday blue laws signed by more than one hundred men. Some of them had gone into the street to survey Minneapolis's saloons and determined they were freely selling alcohol on Sunday. The petition reminded Rand that he, and the police force that was under his control, had the power to enforce the law and ought to do so.[45]

Rand responded quickly. He said he was a temperance man, willing to sacrifice his hopes of eternity if only he could put a stop to the liquor traffic. He also pointed out that there were only ten patrolmen on duty at a time—that was to police the entire city—while there were about two hundred places licensed to sell alcohol. It was impossible to police every infraction of the Sunday ordinance. Nonetheless, arrests were made, and Rand informed every saloonkeeper that the Sunday ordinance would be enforced in the future.

Because many saloons in town stayed closed on Sunday, people left town for their Sunday fun. At that time, the city's southern border was 38th Street, and Minnehaha was well outside Minneapolis city limits. Just as Baker's stone trading house had hosted drinking of uncertain legality in the 1850s, Minnehaha was far enough away that Minneapolis had no claim to policing there.

But when the trains coming back from Minnehaha were absolutely packed with drunk people creating riotous, noisy pandemonium, the railroad told the city's police chief that trains would no longer stop at Minnehaha unless officers were on board to keep order. Though it was beyond the city's jurisdiction, Mayor Rand sent the officers. Minnehaha was, indeed, a dissipated resort.

It's not clear how much of the drunkenness originated at Booth's hotel, how much was Dutch Henry's responsibility, and how much came from other establishments around the falls. But, certainly, those in power seemed to believe that Booth was a respectable man who ran a pleasant and well-kept business. Within a month, he applied for and was granted a liquor license by the county commissioners, who said, "This action will put the control of the liquor traffic into the hands of a responsible party, and get rid of some of the disreputable rum holes of that place. Applications for liquor licenses from Isadore Henry and Albert Henry were rejected." Even after others petitioned on their behalf, the county commission refused.[46]

When Booth opened his hotel in 1880, he promised "to restore the good name of Minnehaha, and to make a resort for ladies and children to come to in perfect safety." Some believed that he had changed the place for the better, but his pledge also sounded very similar to all the previous promises that conviviality would not chaotically rule the premises of the Minnehaha Hotel. As May wound on, Minnehaha, that "scene of some recent combats," was generally peaceable. Booth claimed that disorderliness would not be tolerated, and that those under the influence would be sent away from his grounds. When a couple of "vulgar and profane nuisances" took the train from Minnehaha to the city one evening, the train brakeman—who had tried and failed to keep them under control—kicked them off and gave them a good thrashing. In 1880, orderliness was clearly on the rise at Minnehaha.[47]

Except that Booth had his liquor license rescinded in June. The motion to the county commissioners passed without a dissenting vote. He hadn't had the license even three months. No reason was given for why it was taken from him, but it most likely had something to do with the most common infractions at the time: selling alcohol on Sunday, selling to minors, and public drunkenness.[48]

Toward the end of the 1880 season, Franklin Steele came to visit Minneapolis. He still owned a share in the ground underneath the Minnehaha Hotel, still collected payments from lessees who sold alcohol, and he had other business interests to oversee. He was stricken with paralysis and died quite suddenly, on September 10, 1880. His wife, Annie, died the following January. Their six daughters and two sons inherited the estate of several million dollars and quite a lot of land at and near Minnehaha Falls.[49]

George Lincoln's family left the falls in 1881. This date provides more evidence that the house they lived in belonged to Steele, since Steele's estate was being settled at this time. It also makes sense if they left due to the chaotic nature of the hospitality there. They had some land in town, and they moved to 618 South 16th Street. Captain John Tapper, an early settler who had run the ferry above St. Anthony Falls, eventually moved into the Lincoln house with his wife.[50]

Booth's businesses at the gardens and the hotel provided an outstanding experience of hospitality at the falls. His gardeners, though we do not know their names, did the work to keep the flower beds in glorious bloom. Henry Hines was the hotel cook. A Black man and a widower, he was the person responsible for the fine dinners that Booth was noted for. Also working for Booth at the hotel was Minnie Branch. That name is so perfect that one wonders if it was given to her at birth. Her job was "Jack of All Trades," which surely meant that she changed the sheets, served the meals, washed laundry and dishes, and probably emptied the chamber pots. Minnie was married, though we don't know to whom, and was another Black employee at Booth's. Was Booth making ends meet by hiring Black people at the usual depressed wages? Was he giving hardworking, talented people jobs regardless of their skin color? We don't know.[51]

For four seasons, Booth walked the line between respectable fun and profitable, necessary mayhem. The pleasure of a visit to Minnehaha was not marred by too many reports of public drunkenness. Compared to Donnelly and other proprietors, John Booth paid fewer fines for illegal alcohol sales. He was in many ways the most respectable of the hotelkeepers who operated the Minnehaha Hotel.

Minneapolis was booming. Its population grew from 13,066 in 1870, to 46,887 in 1880, to 164,738 in 1890. In 1883, the city's residents moved to protect some of the open spaces that were quickly disappearing under the demands of the growing population. The legislature passed a bill providing for a Minneapolis park system, and the residents voted to accept it; the Minneapolis Board of Park Commissioners is an independently elected, semi-autonomous body to acquire and maintain city parks. The park board bought and was gifted land for parks and parkways, especially those relating to its plans to keep the city's lakes available to all and to provide healthy open green spaces for its residents to enjoy. Minnehaha Falls was an essential piece of this planning.[52]

4

Four Long Years to Create a Park

I N THE ENTIRE HISTORY OF MINNEAPOLIS, Mayor George A.
Pillsbury's invention of "the dead line" might have been the law
that had the most profound effect on the city's social life. The line—
also known as the "liquor patrol limit" or the "liquor patrol line"—
restricted the licensing of alcohol sales to just a few districts within
the city limits. It became part of the city's official charter in 1884, the
same year Pillsbury was elected, and it wasn't entirely repealed until 2014. This 130-year restriction explains the lack of neighborhood
pubs, saloons, taverns, and watering holes around town. Unless you
lived downtown, or in parts of the West Bank or Northeast neighborhoods, you didn't have a pub. With only a few exceptions, the small
commercial hubs that sprouted up every six blocks along the streetcar
routes never included a place where you could drink.

Minneapolitans eventually grew to accept this strange and limited
state of affairs. Back in the nineteenth century, those forces that were
looking to rein in the public's access to drink, including the editors of
the *Minneapolis Tribune*, saw the law as something that would allow
"this city to free its residence sections absolutely from the curses of
drinking dens and their attendant disorder and crime, and to prevent
the establishment among the homes of the people of these schools
of vice for the degradation of men and the corruption of youth. . . .
The ordinance was well-conceived, well and strongly drawn, well sus-
tained and will be well-enforced."[1]

George Pillsbury was the father of Charles Pillsbury, the flour milling magnate whose name can still be found on grocery store shelves
today. George had come to Minnesota from New Hampshire, following his son to the prosperity the West promised. George Pillsbury

was a conservative Republican, a member of the First Baptist Church of Minneapolis, and a teetotaler. And in his quest to become mayor, he found himself running against Doc Ames, the doctor, surgeon, and Civil War veteran who was running for a third term and who had friends in every saloon.[2]

Albert Alonzo "Doc" Ames had a booming laugh and probably lit up every room he was in. He was also unimpressed with the Yankee social order established by so many of Minneapolis's founders. Unlike Pillsbury, Ames did not use church and business connections to build his network of political support around the city. Ames voters were the workers who made barrels for a few dollars a day, those who came home from the mills covered in flour dust, those who scratched and scraped to get by and often failed. Doc Ames was generous with

Dr. Albert Alonzo
Ames, about 1890.
MNHS

the poor. He even gave the destitute free medical care, saying, "Richer men than you will pay your bill." After returning from a hunting trip with one of the city's policemen, he distributed hundreds of prairie chickens to poor families in town.[3]

Beyond such kindnesses to hardworking people, however, Ames and many of the people who supported or worked for him were, to be honest, on the shady side of things. Never mind that, in 1851, his family was among the earliest claim-stakers in Minneapolis. Never mind that he had a college degree. Ames's crowd included the prostitutes, the gamblers, the shifty criminals, and the drinkers. Politically, he pandered to the saloon owners and encouraged almost every kind of sketchy behavior. He was a carouser, an affable companion disapproved of by the "good" people but beloved in the streets and saloons. As Lincoln Steffens phrased it in his muckraking overview of Minneapolis, he was a "genial generous reprobate."[4]

In the mayoral election of 1884, Pillsbury's line of attack was that the "saloon element was running things," and Ames was letting it happen. At the time, Minneapolis must have been a seething hotbed of unsavory conviviality. It got so bad that even some saloonkeepers disavowed Ames. "His administration has become so thick with sporting men and women, that is, with the gamblers and keepers of houses of ill fame," one said, "that it has become impossible to support him." Some of this dissatisfaction was due to pure economics. In his time as mayor, Ames had enacted a policy known as "low license," which dropped the fee for a liquor permit to a hundred dollars. In just two years of Ames's second term, the number of saloons increased from 252 to 523 licensed businesses, and there weren't enough customers to fill them. Pillsbury saw this as a political opening, and it worked.[5]

Pillsbury proposed his new dead line in his inaugural address in April of 1884. Before the end of the month, the city council had enacted a liquor license ordinance that empowered the mayor to "refuse to grant a license for the sale of liquor in any section of the city he deem fit." The city council, which had a Republican majority, included in the ordinance "high license," which drastically increased the cost of getting licensed to sell liquor. Whereas a license to sell drugs at a pharmacy cost five dollars, a license to sell alcohol now cost five hundred dollars. Outside the dead line, Minneapolis's residential districts suddenly found the areas near their homes spared of the depraved behavior that had so concerned the more decorous Yankee elite.[6]

Pillsbury's new restriction, however, ignored a simple, important truth about alcohol: people like it. And though the temperance movement was vocal in Minneapolis, the public's desire for drink would not be quashed by remonstrations or lack of access. Liquor sales just moved to more secret channels.

WELCOME TO THE BLIND PIG

A "blind pig" was a slang term for an illegal saloon. Unable to afford a five-hundred-dollar liquor license or to set up in certain areas of town, business owners around Minneapolis began selling alcohol through candy stores, confectionaries, and any other kinds of back-alley arrangements one might imagine. In many of these places, drinks were served by an "invisible bartender." You'd walk up to a counter, put your coin in a slot (a literal hole in the wall), and a sliding panel would open, revealing a hand serving you a glass of beer, a shot of whiskey, or maybe a whiskey drink known as red lemonade.[7]

Illegal alcohol sales were part and parcel of life, not just in Minneapolis but everywhere in Hennepin County. This meant, of course, that the ongoing problems at Minnehaha got worse.

Down by the falls, John Booth had stopped managing the Minnehaha Hotel in 1883. By this time, he was in his fifties and had been doing hard physical work for years. His wife, a woman named Emma, had urged him to invest in a saloon in downtown Minneapolis. Exchanging the grueling work of maintaining a hotel, greenhouse, and gardens for a simple saloon operation might have come as a relief.

Booth sold the lease on the Minnehaha Hotel to Lewis J. Clark, from Sioux Falls, South Dakota. Clark continued running an illegal saloon on the premises and proved to be much more flagrant about flouting the law than Booth—or Hugh Donnelly before him—had ever been. As one newspaper reported, after he took over the hotel, "decent people" had been driven away by "a couple of gin mills with a dance-house attachment," and Minnehaha had been "abandoned to the roughs. . . . The place has lost its charm, and will probably never regain it."[8]

At that time, Richfield Township held jurisdiction over the falls, and its residents were encouraged by the way "the saloons on the outskirts [of Minneapolis] have been abandoned," as the *Minneapolis Tribune* put it in 1884. Trying to control the flow of alcohol and the mayhem often left in its wake, Richfield had again voted for "no license." But that had only resulted in blind pigs popping up everywhere, with the ongoing transgressions at Minnehaha serving as particularly glaring examples. The public had cycled back into one of those moments where a majority believed that "this fair spot of nature has been desecrated and the laws unheeded," and Richfield's concerned citizenry put together a committee, went to the falls to collect information, and built their case. Booth, who at that point was still running his refreshment pavilion at the gardens, was arrested but got off relatively easy; he only had to pay a few dollars in court costs and promise to quit his illegal business. Isadore Henry and his wife from the Minnehaha Spring Garden Hotel were both arrested. Henry was also arrested a second and then a third time, just for good measure. He kept claiming that he hadn't sold any spiritous liquors for a year, that he'd quit the business and didn't know it was being sold at his hotel, that he didn't know who kept the bar, and that he owned the building and grounds but did not know a saloon was being run there. All these claims were proved false. And when his underage daughter was found guilty of selling alcohol, the court fined Henry and his wife fifty dollars each.[9]

Lewis Clark was arrested. The Richfield committee brought a total of sixteen cases against him, and he panicked a bit. After getting an extension for his hearing, he tried bargaining with the court. He suggested closing his bar (except to a few trusted friends). He offered to collect all the liquor, lock it away, and stop selling it, though his proposal included storing it at the hotel. He said he would find someone else to rent the saloon section of the hotel. All of these offers were clearly supposed to help get him off the hook, but none of them would help solve the bigger problem of drunk people carousing at Minnehaha Falls.

The court finally insisted that Clark conduct no saloon business himself nor permit any such business on his property. He eventually asked for time to speak with Vinette Lincoln, to see if he could be freed from his lease at the hotel. The newspaper thought that "the persuasive voice of Justice Grimes oft repeating the touching words, '$75 and costs,' will mellow his heart and turn his erring steps."[10]

ENTER THE BOARD OF TRADE: WHAT'S WANTED IS A PARK

Both the Republicans' political ascendency in Minneapolis and the new dead line law had encouraged Richfield Township to do its house-cleaning at the falls, and soon, the Minneapolis Board of Trade took up the idea of turning Minnehaha Falls into a park.

It wasn't the first time. Discussions about converting the area into a park went back at least as far as 1868. Thirteen years after *The Song of Hiawatha* was published, the poem had turned Minnehaha into a celebrated attraction. The *Tribune*, endorsing the call for the creation of a park, noted that hundreds of thousands of visitors from all over the world, and the uncountable others who had read the poem, all felt a deep longing "to see 'the laughing water' as it danced to its fall in its sequestered spot in the heart of the great North American continent."[11]

In the 1860s, Franklin Steele's refreshment house attracted crowds over the well-worn road that led to the cascade. Minnehaha was treated as a common attraction, which led the local newspaper to remind visitors that preserving the picturesque beauty of the place was an important task: "We have all of us been guilty of neglect towards Minnehaha in not taking it under our fostering care long ago. Let all be of one mind concerning our duty in the premises."

This longing to preserve a picturesque Minnehaha was a response to a more profound sentiment in the air. Americans were seeing the effects of industrialization and the ways new technologies were re-making the land. Great losses were visible in every direction. Whole forests were vanishing into the grinding blades of sawmills, prairies were being uprooted and replaced with wheat fields, and the air and water were becoming dangerously filthy. Congress created the first national park at Yellowstone in 1872 and preserved another particu-larly picturesque site, Yosemite, in 1874.

American cities all had neighborhoods where poor workers crowded into dingy tenement buildings and where illnesses like typhoid, yellow fever, and tuberculosis ran rampant. In urban areas, people longed for access to green, open spaces. In New York, the desire for green space became so great that Green-Wood Cemetery in Brooklyn came to serve as a park (eventually inspiring the creation of Central Park in Manhattan). Minneapolis's Lakewood Cemetery, founded in 1871, was created on the model of Spring Grove Cemetery in Cincinnati. Lakewood was designed to provide beautiful, open grounds where the city's residents could stroll and contemplate.[12]

Both Minneapolis and St. Paul had sprung up on sites that were a good distance away from Fort Snelling; Minneapolis is eight river miles upstream at St. Anthony Falls, and St. Paul is six miles downstream, at what many call the head of practical navigation. People began pouring into Minnesota in the 1860s. Both cities were growing rapidly, and it seemed it would only be a matter of time before they met at the confluence of the rivers, the fort, and Minnehaha. In the face of this encroachment, it was well understood that this graceful, picturesque waterfall should be cherished, preserved, and protected. The natural environment was receding. Creating a park, especially in a place of such particular beauty, was the best chance to preserve a small bit of what was being lost.[13]

In 1868, St. Paul's Chamber of Commerce made initial attempts to make Minnehaha Park a reality by passing a resolution stating that the US Congress should set aside 2,500 acres on both sides of the river—four sections of the military reservation—for a public park. (At the time, the federal government was still enmeshed in negotiations with Franklin Steele over payments for and ownership of this land.) The resolution didn't exactly describe which four sections should be set aside, but it was known that the creek's north side was already in private hands, and the plan didn't include that "most picturesque spot: the high bluff to the north at the mouth of the creek." Ard Godfrey no doubt read that line with some interest. After all, that was his land.[14]

Though this initial effort quietly faded away, in 1875, the park idea was revived by a joint meeting of both cities' committees on parks, which represented the Minneapolis Board of Trade and the Chambers of Commerce for both Minneapolis and St. Paul. These civic organizations allowed the two cities' powerful and wealthy businessmen to have a crucial impact on the park's eventual construction; without them, there would be no park at all. In the meeting's original plans, the new space would be called the Union Park, and it would include Minnehaha Falls as well as a permanent site for the state fairgrounds. The park would be sited on both sides of the Mississippi River. Neither city had a budget to buy the land at the time, and the consensus was that the proposed location was too remote from both cities to be practical. So the idea failed.[15]

Almost a decade later, in December of 1884, with the dead line for liquor sales in place, Minneapolis's Board of Trade took up the idea again, passing a resolution that asked the state legislature to condemn the land around Minnehaha for use as a park. People were still looking for a permanent home for the state fairgrounds. Minneapolis liked the idea of siting the fair at Minnehaha, which offered the added enticement of the waterfall, though St. Paul was leaning toward the Ramsey County Poor Farm, which had the chief virtue of being flat.[16]

With a head of steam stoked by the intercity rivalry over the fairgrounds, the citizens of Minneapolis became more keenly aware that the creation of Minnehaha Park—still outside the city's limits—was a truly desirable idea. The *Minneapolis Daily Tribune* reported, "Not a man in Minneapolis dissents from the proposition that Minnehaha ought to be a public park. . . . This piece of property ought not to belong to private individuals." It cannot have hurt the effort that the two biggest landowners at the falls, Franklin Steele and George Lincoln, had both recently died.[17]

The initial resolution looked solid, so in January of 1885, the Minneapolis Board of Trade got busy drafting legislation. During this era, nothing important happened in the city without first forming a commission to work on the problem, and the Board of Trade's bill created a state park commission. It was made up of five men tasked with identifying as many as a thousand acres in Hennepin or Ramsey County that could be condemned for the use of Minnesota's first state park. They were to begin by having the land surveyed, then publish a map so that landowners and others with a stake in the property could respond. A separate committee of appraisers would determine how much the landowners should get for their property. The Fourth District Court was assigned to confirm the work of both the park commission and the appraisers, and the bill allowed any interested party to appeal to the state supreme court. Finally, if the legislature, in 1887 or 1889, failed to appropriate any money to pay for the park's

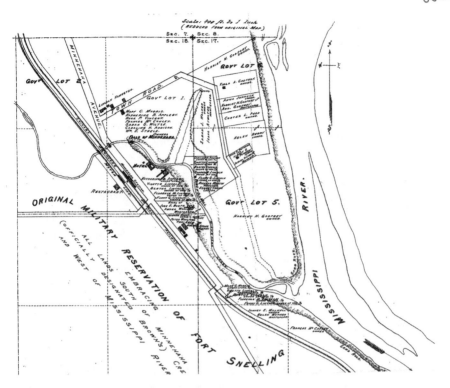

The state park commission's 1885 map of the area that would become the park.
"GOVT LOT 5" was Ard Godfrey's claim. *Hennepin County property records*

construction, the entire enterprise would collapse, leaving the land in
private hands. After a few minor tweaks, this was the bill that made
its way to the state legislature.[18]

The ins and outs of the Minnesota state legislature might be just
as stultifying as the history of railroad financing in the nineteenth
century. But the most important element—the money quote from
the whole state park bill—was this: the park was defined for "agricultural, horticultural, and mechanical state exhibit grounds and for
the location of other state institutions and buildings." The intent, of
course, was to create an opportunity to host the fair at Minnehaha
Falls, which actually wasn't a bad idea. The *Minneapolis Tribune* rallied
for the idea, supporting another provision in the bill that stated the
park could also include Minnesota's new state capitol. At the time,
the capitol building was a temporary affair (it would be built anew
beginning in 1896). Clearly, the seat of state government deserved a

more exalted location, and a Union Park on both sides of the river, with Minnehaha Falls included, would have been ideal. The bill was introduced in the legislature just four days after the Board of Trade discussed the draft in their meeting.

∽

The state fair's location was quickly and irrevocably settled in that same month of January 1885, when Ramsey County offered to give the Ramsey County Poor Farm property to the state agricultural society. With that decision finalized, the legislature returned to the idea of turning Minnehaha into Minnesota's first state park, and on February 28, they passed the park bill, this time settling on a size of two hundred acres.[19]

Even with the Minneapolis Board of Trade lending its legal talents to the effort, the idea that the bill was going to create Minnesota's first "state" park was something of a fiction. The new park was never going to be anywhere but Minnehaha—the bill made that clear—and Minnehaha Park has never been under the state's jurisdiction. After the process for the park's creation was underway in 1887, Minneapolis's city limits were extended to 54th Street South. That extension, of course, gave Minneapolis's city government jurisdiction over this area (and it's still part of Minneapolis today).

In the spring of 1885, the five state park commissioners met. The commission included members from St. Paul, Winona, and Litchfield, as well as two members from the Minneapolis park board: George A. Brackett and commission president Charles Loring. At the end of June, Loring—later to be revered as "the father of Minneapolis Parks"—invited thirty-five guests to take the steamboat *Henry W. Longfellow* from St. Paul to the levee built by Ard Godfrey at the mouth of the creek. The weather was as perfect as could be. It was sunny but not too hot, and rain the previous week had made everything look fresh, green, and inviting. The waterfall was flowing nicely. Along with the commissioners and their wives, the group included the prominent landscape architect Horace W. S. Cleveland.[20]

Horace Cleveland would have had much to say about preserving the natural environment. The wild beauty of the Mississippi River gorge between the fort and Minneapolis today has largely been preserved because of Cleveland's informed voice, his persistence, and his vision. (It was Cleveland who proposed that Minneapolis create the interconnected series of parks, including Minnehaha, that came to be known as the Grand Rounds—and preserves shoreline property around most of the city's lakes.)

After disembarking at the levee at the mouth of the creek, the group walked three-quarters of a mile upstream through the shady glen, taking Godfrey's mill access road. It is still there today, a lane along the north side of the creek, wide enough for a horse and wagon to deliver to the mill, or (now) wide enough for park maintenance vehicles or park police cars. Undoubtedly, the group discussed the murmuring of the creek, the steep-sided gorge through which it runs, the cool shade of the natural environment, the birds, and the loveliness of it all.

Upon reaching the waterfall, the guests enjoyed the scenery while the commissioners held their meeting. Having all been to the falls before, they already had opinions about what the park's boundaries should be. Now, with the actual land before them and a map in hand, they confirmed the borders for themselves, basically sketching out the triangular-shaped park we still know today and settling very close to the two-hundred-acre limit the legislature had specified for the park. All of this activity was in their remit; the only thing the commission couldn't do was appropriate the necessary funds for the park's construction.

The commissioners also took a look at the businesses operating in the area surrounding the falls. The *Minneapolis Tribune* was thoroughly in favor of the park idea, of course, and it saw the commercial establishments as a blight. "The use that the public has so far made of the falls has certainly done nothing to enhance their value," the paper wrote, "and those buildings which have been erected near them are not altogether such as a lover of nature can admire." The Minnehaha Hotel loomed over the waterfall's south edge, visible to all, even those making the perilous trip behind the water. Those same grounds also held various smaller buildings, stables, fences, and Booth's hurdy-gurdy swing and roller coaster. The tourists all wanted their pictures taken with the waterfall as their backdrop, so whoever was in charge of the hotel leased the photograph concession stand precariously perched on the edge of the Minnehaha gorge, which included a dark-room right on the platform. As the author of an 1881 tourist guide

The photographer's platform marred the side of the glen, about 1875. *Photo by C. B. Chase*

wistfully noted: "Before the side of the glen was marred by the platform that now decorates its side, it was a place where one could forget that there was an outside world of noise and work and care, and the simple beauty of the murmuring cascade, with its numberless rainbows shimmering in the sunlight, gave one a feeling of rest that was delicious." Minnehaha had turned cheap and commercial.[21]

For how many decades had the public been promised redemption at Minnehaha? For how long had they been expecting a return to the respect due to—as the *Tribune* put it—"the falls which nature has given to man, of which the state of Minnesota is no more than a chance trustee"? The poem that had made the waterfall famous was

Charlotte Ouisconsin Van Cleve, the daughter of an army officer, was not yet two months old when she arrived at Fort Snelling in 1819. She grew up there, and in 1888 she reminisced about the Minnehaha Falls she knew as a girl.

The most charming of all our recreations was a ride to "Little Falls" now "Minnehaha." The picture in my mind of this gem of beauty, makes the sheet of water wider and more circular than it is now, I know it was fresher and newer, and there was no saloon there then, no fence, no tables and benches, cut up and disfigured with names and nonsense, no noisy railroad, no hotel, it was just our dear pure "Little Falls" with its graceful ferns, its bright flowers, its bird music and its lovely water-fall. And while we children rambled on the banks, and gathered pretty fragrant things fresh from their Maker's hand, listening the while to sweet sounds in the air, and to the joyous liquid music of the laughing water, there may have been some love-making going on in the cozy nooks and corners on the hill side or under the green trees, for in later years, I have now and then come upon groups of two, scattered here and there in those same places, who looked like lovers, which recalled to my mind vividly what I had seen there long ago.

That enchanting spot, so dainty in its loveliness, is hallowed by a thousand tender associations and it seems more than cruel to allow its desecration by unholy surroundings and various forms of vice. Standing beside it now, and remembering it in its purity, just as God made it, my eyes are full of unshed tears, and its mellifluous ceaseless song seems pleading to be saved from the vandalism which threatens to destroy all its sweet influences and make it common and unclean. But as I, alone, of all who saw it in those days long gone by, stand mourning by its side, there dawns in my heart the hope that the half formed purpose now talked of, for making it the centre of a park for the delight of the two cities between which it stands, may be perfected, thus saving it from destruction and making this bright jewel in its setting of green, the very queen of all the many attractions of this part of our State. Surely no spot in ours or any other State offers such beauty or so many inducements for such a purpose, and coming generations will forever bless the men who shall carry it out, thus preserving our lovely Minnehaha and the charming surroundings for their own delight and the enjoyment of those who shall come after them.[v]

now thirty years old. So many readers still cherished it, but there was also a growing sentiment that Minnehaha should be more than just a beautiful local spot that had unexpectedly become famous through Longfellow's words. It should also be beloved for its own merits. It managed to be both grand and accessible; it was cool, shady, wild, storied, and close to home. Sometimes thunderous, sometimes a bit more than a ripple, Minnehaha was, at the time of the park's creation, firmly situated at Minnesota's very heart.[22]

When the commission announced the park's likely boundaries, they also alerted the landowners that their time near the falls would soon be over. The children of Franklin and Annie Steele had inherited their land near the falls, but most of them no longer lived in Minnesota. The Godfreys were still living on their land on the proposed tract's eastern edge, and a few other people owned smaller parcels. George Lincoln had died, and his widow, Vinette, and their three daughters had inherited his land. Of all these landowners, Vinette Lincoln would go on to have the most to say about the park's creation—and its later operations.

THE CLINK OF BEER BOTTLES AND THE HIGH HAND OF MORAL BEHAVIOR

That same lovely June, as the commissioners were deciding the boundaries of the new Minnehaha Park, things were no more respectable at the falls than they had been the year before, when Richfield Township had attempted to clean house. Lurching drunks, lewd women, and vulgar behavior continued. Illegal alcohol sales were still going on, both at the hotel and at Dutch Henry's Place. The sentiment that something had to change was nearly universal. In June of 1885, an anonymous tirade appeared in multiple newspapers around town:

> Minneapolis has one world-famous piece of scenery whose beauty has been sung in poetry, whose legend the country's greatest poet has woven into one of his best and most popular productions. No traveler of education visiting the city omits Minnehaha. What do we of this city think of it? We think it is one of our lowest resorts, almost the last place we would visit on Sunday for the day and have it be known. The

clink of beer bottles has smothered the "laughing" of the falls. The frequenters turn their backs to the water as they lift aloft the foaming cup that contains anything but water. Where formerly there was peace now is the boisterous roller coaster, the 5 cent whirling swing, and the modest conversation of "tough" people from the city. In the midst of it all is a flagrant saloon defying the law. A pretty picture, and each year growing worse.[23]

Contrary to the anonymous author's appraisal, for many people, Minnehaha was not a place of last resort; it was an extremely popular destination. The early steam streetcar, known as the motor line, carried carloads of people to the falls on the weekends, and even more took the railroad. The roads were lined with buggies and carriages full of visitors. Business was so good for Harriet Collar, who opened her restaurant at the falls that summer, that she had to advertise for a "girl waiter" for Sundays and a woman to clean. Business was also good for two other women. After going to the falls and visiting the blind pig, "Belle Chester" and "Maude Dillon" were charged with "disorderly conduct"—a bit of a catchall phrase that, when applied to women, meant prostitution. Their conduct got them arrested and fined seven dollars and fifty cents each. At the time, Minneapolis dealt with prostitution by requiring the women involved to make monthly court appearances and pay recurring fines, just as part of their business operations.[24]

In December of 1885, the landowners and leaseholders knew what was coming. The commission had come up with park boundaries that included their land. Perhaps they wanted to see how long they could hold out. But the high hand of moral behavior came down like a fist at Minnehaha Falls. Someone burned the Minnehaha Hotel to the ground.

The building was closed for the season and unoccupied, but somehow, the fire broke out in a room on an upper floor on the hotel's south side before sweeping north through the building. Everything burned: the little roller coaster, the hurdy-gurdy swing, a small store, and a few outbuildings. Even the fence—which was a good distance from the hotel at the edge of the property—was destroyed. The only thing left untouched was the photographer's platform at the falls.

The steam-powered streetcar known as the motor line carried Minneapolitans to Minnehaha Falls, about 1883. *Published by American Scenery*

Most people thought it had to be arson, but since the building wasn't insured, there was no investigation. At the time, Lewis Clark still held the lease on the property, and he was out thousands of dollars for the furniture inside the building.[25]

❧

Doc Ames became mayor again in April of 1886. Pillsbury didn't want to run for a second term, and it took the Republicans weeks to maneuver and then actually nominate him without his consent to get him to appear on the ballot. The *Minneapolis Tribune* was as viciously anti-Ames as it was pro-Pillsbury. "All parts of the city were corrupted with the flaunting vice and drunkenness and 'sporting' of the [previous] Ames administration," the *Tribune* claimed, and it urged voters to stay the course. "Another term accorded to Mayor Pillsbury will permanently establish the principles of high license and patrol limits." The *St. Paul Globe,* which ran many more column inches about the contest, was defiantly pro-Ames. They rallied the Scandinavian vote against Pillsbury, painting him as a candidate who said that workingmen were all foreigners whose votes were for sale. Because high license had squeezed out the smaller saloons and forced them into illegal operations—the dead line had created blind pigs in every grocery store in town, it seemed—the prohibitionists eventually turned on Pillsbury, too. Ultimately, Ames's working-class army of supporters put him back in office with a margin of over five thousand votes.[26]

THE SOLDIERS' HOME, OR THE LOST FIFTY ACRES OF MINNEHAHA PARK

The park's creation ultimately took four years, and between 1885, when the state park bill passed, and 1889, when the title was finally acquired, the process proved a disaster for Minnehaha Park. Over eleven months in 1887, fifty acres of the park were given away forever. The story demonstrates the political power of Civil War veterans— and, perhaps, the community's priorities.

Over two million people served in the Union Army during the Civil War, and in 1886, former soldiers formed the Grand Army of the Republic (GAR) to honor their shared experience. The GAR grew to include hundreds of thousands of Civil War veterans. Over many years, the group held encampments where the old soldiers reconvened and paraded in formation through the streets, reexperiencing the homecoming cheers they had heard when they returned from the war. During one of the national encampments convened in Minneapolis, 100,000 people watched the old soldiers go by.[27]

Though the GAR primarily began as a way for soldiers to build camaraderie, it developed political muscle as the veterans of "the late unpleasantness" advocated for and won pensions for themselves. And in the 1880s, two decades after the war, a national upwelling of sentiment grew for the soldiers who were becoming middle-aged—and for some who had fallen on hard, hard times. A number of soldiers had returned from the war with wounds that did not heal. Their injuries might have been called soldier's heart; today we recognize them as post-traumatic stress disorder (PTSD). Almshouses and poorhouses, those places of last refuge for the indigent and penniless, counted these veterans among their number. Simply put, care for these people was a disgrace.

When the GAR decided to focus its attention on the shame and pain of neglected veterans, the idea of building homes for old soldiers took on a sense of national urgency. The group's ideas weren't novel; at least some Revolutionary War veterans were awarded pensions, and the first Old Soldiers' Home was opened in 1851 in Washington, DC. But the GAR's political muscle helped put the necessary energy behind the development of the national soldiers' home movement in the late nineteenth century.

The Minnesota chapter of the GAR brought the question to the state legislature in 1887, seeking $100,000 to build a Minnesota Soldiers' Home. The legislature appropriated just $50,000 to pay for the site. Because forming a commission was vital to get anything done, Governor Andrew R. McGill appointed a commission to select a site in the spring of 1887. The home could be located anywhere in Minnesota, and the commissioners toured Austin, Litchfield, St. Cloud, and Red Wing. Redwood Falls offered a site; so did Lake City and Waseca. A place on Lake Minnetonka was also considered. Minneapolis or St. Paul, however, were considered to be the top options. Representative John B. Gilfillan introduced a bill in Congress to set aside twenty acres of the ever-shrinking Fort Snelling military reservation for the soldiers' home.[28]

The soldiers' home commission moved as quickly as the state park commission did not. There was no site in either Minneapolis or St. Paul that the commission could acquire without securing additional cash from the city. The St. Paul Chamber of Commerce weighed in again in June with the old idea of a Union Park that spanned both sides of the river. Since the creation of Minnehaha Park was underway, they planned to purchase and develop some land across the river from it and call it Hiawatha Park, which would serve as a complement to the soldiers' home. They even had some money to pay for it. (It is not clear whether anyone pointed out that this area at Hidden Falls included the site of Joe Brown's Rum Town.)[29]

Doc Ames, himself a Civil War veteran and GAR man, agitated for the home to be located at the mouth of Minnehaha Creek. He wrote to the commission: "On behalf of the people of the city of Minneapolis

I offer as a site for the proposed soldiers' home a tract of fifty acres of land in the city of Minneapolis, situated on the west bank of the Mississippi River, near Minnehaha Falls, and valued at $75,000. If the proposition is accepted I feel authorized in stating that said grounds will be connected with the present park systems of Minneapolis and St. Paul in such a manner as to make it the most attractive and beautiful spot in the state. Very respectfully, A. A. Ames, Mayor."[30]

Ames was able to make this offer because when the city boundaries expanded south to include the waterfall, he had acquired jurisdiction

Ard Godfrey's claim, about 1887. Photographer L. Mel Hyde stood on the old Godfrey claim looking upriver, before the construction of the Ford Bridge and Lock and Dam #1. This beautiful vista is one reason the site was chosen for the Minnesota Soldiers' Home.

over the location. But he must have persuaded Ard and Harriet God-frey to agree to this idea as well, since the fifty acres under consider-ation had been their land since they claimed it in 1852.

Ames surely knew that the park's proposed map included those fifty acres and that they were supposed to be part of Minnehaha Park; the map of the park had been on file for more than a year. Ames also must have known that there were other places on the riverbank be-tween the fort and Minneapolis that were available for the soldiers' home. But he still just scooped up part of the proposed park and of-fered it to the soldiers' home commission.

While it's not entirely clear why Ames made this decision, city politics offer some clues. The state park commission was controlled by Republicans who had no love for him. They had seen his man-agement style over two administrations and were staring down the barrel of a third. While the state park commission had no direct effect on the mayor's office, the Republican power brokers at the Board of Trade did, and they spun up what the *Globe* called a "back room de-vice"—naturally, it was another commission, this one overseeing the Minneapolis police. Created through an act of the state legislature, it was supposedly nonpartisan, but it had been heartily endorsed by the anti-Ames *Minneapolis Tribune*, which claimed this new police commission was needed because "at present the policemen of Min-neapolis are not allowed to enforce the laws. They have been obliged by their superiors to extend immunity to the gamblers and swindling fakirs that infest the city, and they protect violators of the liquor and Sunday laws." They said that Ames should resign, and they went so far as to print that he was "spoiling a first-class surgeon to make a very bad mayor."[31]

With the commission now overseeing the force, Ames no longer exerted direct control over the police, a move he deeply resented. He said, "In my opinion this high-handed partisan fanatical legislation against the will of the people will give us a Democratic governor and legislature two years from now, when the evils now being inflicted will meet with speedy revocation." Ames carried grudges, and his de-cision about the acreage intended for the park could have been the product of this one. He was also vain, and he might have seen the sol-diers' home location in his city as a way to extend his own influence.[32]

Even with Ames's promise of the acres to site the home, how to pay for this parcel of land was an issue. The soldiers' home commission bill had provided only $10,000, so Ames turned to the city council and convinced them to throw in $30,000 more. The Board of Trade, with its formidable conservative businessmen, also formed a committee to collect donations. Their initial effort attracted just $5,000, however. Since many of those wealthy businessmen were seemingly opposed to Ames's administration, it's no surprise that the requests didn't garner a lot of support. The donations came from men who owned the land nearest Godfrey's and nearest the falls; they were expecting the value to go up so that they could sell and make a profit. Canvassing for more subscribers was going to be important. The committee planned to secure "whatever is needed as no public project has awakened such general enthusiasm as a movement to establish a home . . . a place where the old and helpless heroes of the war can pass their declining days with comfort, not as burdens upon the state but as charges of a grateful people." That's an inspiring idea, but not truthful. Almost none of the money donated to the soldiers' home effort came through small public donations.[33]

The soldiers' home commission began voting on the site selection in June. Because the members came from all over the state, there was little consensus among them about the Minnehaha site—even though the GAR rank and file were happy with the idea, the Minneapolis Board of Trade was working to secure funds, and the St. Paul Chamber of Commerce was working on Hiawatha Park across the river. But nothing was certain. Between June and July of 1887, the commission voted over ninety times without coming to a decision. After agreeing that a four-vote majority would be enough to settle the home's location, they took one last vote. Minnehaha triumphed.[34]

A month later, thousands of GAR men and their families from all over the state converged on the site to see what it was like. In the end, the rank-and-file members walked the grounds and heartily approved of the location. So did the *Tribune*, which noted, "The sunset gun and bugle will renew [the veteran's] patriotism every day." Both Mayor Ames and Governor McGill gave speeches.[35]

But in the back of everyone's mind was the fact that this carefully selected location still was not yet paid for. The site selection vote had also come with a number of caveats. The resolution that won out, which included Ames's offer that the city would come up with the money to buy the land, was time-limited to two months and would expire on September 10. The clock was ticking. "However," the *Globe* cheerfully reported, "there is no doubt in the minds of those who know that the money will be raised." The city council was on the hook for $30,000, and the landowners who subscribed early had only contributed about $5,000. For want of another $15,000 from Minneapolis's citizens, the site might be lost. This was the state of play on August 23. There were seventeen days left to raise the money.[36]

A solicitation was signed by everyone on the Board of Trade committee, a number of GAR post commanders, more landowners in the area around Minnehaha, and Charles M. Loring, directly appealing to the public: "Citizens of Minneapolis must put hands in pockets and come up with the money for [the] soldiers' home." As the deadline approached, St. Paul's park commission added to the excitement for placing the soldiers' home at Minnehaha when they condemned about fifty acres to create the companion park across the river. Despite any initial ideas, it was not called Union Park or Hiawatha Park, though. Today it is known as Hidden Falls Park, and (beyond proximity) it has only a faint connection to Minnehaha.[37]

On September 3, a week before the deadline, the Board of Trade still had not raised the needed cash, and Mayor Ames appealed directly to the city council, asking if they could just supply the needed $55,000. The council unanimously agreed to do so.

Ultimately, they did not have to give the whole amount. At the last possible moment, the committee came up with the funds. The money came from twenty wealthy men who were on the lookout for a way to make money, investing in the land nearby. And they didn't *give* the funds; they *loaned* them. The group took out two loans that added up to $55,000, one at seven percent and one at eight percent, both for eighteen months. A few of the signatories, like Doc Ames and Charles W. Johnson, were veterans, but most were not. The real estate investors close to the falls happily signed on. And the city council agreed to go to the legislature to ask for an appropriation to repay the two loans.[38]

As for the math on this endeavor, there's a very kind action buried in the twists and turns of the tale. The original Board of Trade request for funds had netted donations of $5,000. The two notes signed by the twenty wealthy men added $55,000 to the mix, so they had raised a total of $60,000. Ames's original letter had suggested that the fifty acres for the soldiers' home were worth $75,000. His letter did not describe the exact parcel, but it was understood to be Ard Godfrey's claim on the north side of the creek. As the deadline got closer, a GAR man named Major R. R. Henderson brokered the deal with the Godfreys. Harriet Godfrey, who legally owned the land on the peninsula, accepted $60,000 for her fifty acres and then returned $10,000 of it to the soldiers' home commission "as a token of their appreciation of the services of the soldiers and sailors who fought in the Rebellion of 1861."[39]

Loring, the president of the state park commission, had also signed the solicitation to raise the money to place the soldiers' home at Minnehaha. One might wonder why. The answer seems to be that he didn't have any choice but to accept the commission's decision. This strange twist of fate was provided in the state park bill itself, which noted the park was to be used for "agricultural, horticultural, and mechanical state exhibit grounds and for the location of other state institutions and buildings." But what did Loring think about this sudden new use for the picturesque site of the beautiful, famous waterfall? Well, he didn't contribute to the cause. The other man who was both a Minneapolis park board member and a member of the state park commission was George A. Brackett, and he did.[40]

The Godfreys' gift of $10,000 to the commission allowed developers to start planning and building dormitory buildings, a dining hall, and a hospital to care for the indigent and needy veterans. It was autumn of 1887. The entire process of acquiring the land for the soldiers' home, from bill to commission to site, was completed in under eleven months. The place was secured, but the permanent buildings needed to be designed and constructed. In the meantime, interim housing had to be found.

Around this same time, Dutch Henry was trying with little success to lease the Minnehaha Spring Garden Hotel to another businessman. The soldiers' home commission likely saw leasing his place as a win for their side. It would relieve Minnehaha of a persistent source of illegal alcohol and the rowdyism that followed in its wake. And it would also house the soldiers close to the beloved Minnehaha Falls; to Fort Snelling, where these soldiers had mustered into the service; and to the eventual site of the soldiers' home. Henry's Place could

Dutch Henry's dance hall, bedecked with the Minnesota Soldiers' Home banner, about 1887; the building to the right is his old Minnehaha Spring Garden Hotel. *Bromley Collection, HCL*

be had for an incredibly low price to boot, and soon enough, Dutch Henry's old dance hall was turned into a dormitory.[41]

Either John Booth's house or his greenhouse (reports vary) was used as the veterans' hospital. After leaving to run the saloon downtown, Booth had kept his greenhouse operation, along with its refreshment pavilion, going for another year or two. But things in his life were quickly declining. Booth was drinking too much, and his wife, Emma, was encouraging him in it. He died in January of 1886.[42]

Other buildings on the properties around the falls were also used for temporary housing, and before winter, fifty residents were staying in the temporary soldiers' home. They needed medical care, of course, and the doctor who got the job was Doc Ames, who had always been loved by the downtrodden and by the veterans as one of their own.[43]

BUT WHAT ABOUT THE PARK?

After all this, there still was no park, because there was still no money for it. In 1886, the appraisers for the parkland were finally selected and ready to look at the acreage in October. When they announced their findings in 1887, everyone took it to court, following the provisions in the park bill. The objections in the Fourth District courtroom exploded like fireworks. The landowners and lessees all had the same complaints: it was unfair, unconstitutional, and unjust, and the commission had no jurisdiction over the land! The appraisers had established a total valuation of $88,736.52 for what land remained after the Godfrey land was taken, but the landowners said that still wasn't enough. Nearby land had sold for $5,000 an acre, so how could park appraisers expect the owners to settle for a fifth of that or even less? (That claim of $5,000, by the way, was unrealistic; even the Godfrey land had sold for just about a thousand dollars an acre.) Their properties were between two great cities, they were "about one of the most noted curiosities of the world," and they "have special values because of their availability for hotel and garden purposes."[44]

The state legislature appropriated nothing for Minnehaha in 1887. By this time, the landowners had had enough time to organize and figure out their legal options. In the first week in October, 1887, the Steele heirs, along with Vinette Lincoln and her daughters, Harriet Collar, John Booth's children, and some others—a total of twenty-six people—appealed the Fourth District Court's decision on the land valuations, sending the case to the state supreme court. It was all to no avail. The following March, the higher court upheld the original appraisals.[45]

The 1889 legislative session was the last chance to capture the park and the waterfall. The *Tribune* reminded everyone that the city should pay for the parkland if the state wasn't willing to. It was a maddeningly slow process.[46]

The state park commissioners filed their final report to the state legislature on February 5, 1889. The commission had done every task assigned to them by the park bill in 1885. They had established the park's boundaries, discovered the titles, appraised the land, and settled challenges to the appraisals. The report was placed on file.[47]

The very next day, lawyers representing the landowners visited the state legislature's judiciary committee, which was considering a bill to repeal the state park act. The argument, as ever, was over the land's value. The owners argued they had not gotten justice in the courts and so they had brought their appeal to the legislature. Vinette Lincoln said that not only was her offered appraisal lower than the price she had been offered recently, it was lower than the $525 per acre George had paid for the land in 1873. Others told similar stories.[48]

The judiciary committee was also treated to the booming voice of Judge Seagrave Smith of Minneapolis, who was there to speak on behalf of the landowners. Smith let forth with the same arguments they'd tried in the Fourth District Court in 1887. "It's robbery, gentlemen!" he cried. "Robbery! It is not just. It's not right to put your hands in these people's pockets and steal their land."

Months later, on September 12, a number of aldermen (later known as city council members), park board members, members of the state park and soldiers' home commissions, landscape architect Horace Cleveland, and miscellaneous others turned up at a judiciary committee hearing to argue that the appraisals should stand. For the park board, R. G. Evans argued that to repeal the park act would be an injustice to the men who had bought land nearby in good faith, expecting its value to go up. (A more craven attempt to line their pockets is hard to imagine, and this argument shows how the park board favored the wealthy elite landowners. In fact, one of these landowners was a real estate man from Maine named Albert J. Boardman—who was, in 1889, a commissioner on the park board.) The park board provided two suggestions toward resolving the situation. The first was to adopt the state park commission report, which had been sitting in a file for the last eight months. The second mandated that the governor convey title to the city of Minneapolis. They then presented two bills to this effect.[49]

Professor Cleveland spoke about the perfection of the falls and the area for a park, and Seagrave Smith spoke again in defense of the landowners. The state's actions were no better than stealing, he said, reiterating a now-familiar argument. He spoke with passion about his clients' willingness to exhaust every last legal option before they would submit. Another lawyer for the landowners, E. W. Huffcutt, rebutted an earlier comment from R. G. Evans, who had alluded to the seedy character of people who had frequented the falls in previous years. This made things personal because Vinette Lincoln, who was one of the claimants, owned the hotel. In defending her, Huffcutt challenged the room to make more charges if they had them yet to make. Evans recanted, saying, "I simply alluded to what I had been told as to the character of the place." But Huffcutt was still breathing fire. "It would be better and more honorable," he said, "and I challenge those who go about with these whisperings to come boldly and make charges. A covert attack has been made on one of the owners of this property!"

Evans tried to calm things, but Huffcutt would have none of it. Finally, Evans rose to his feet, towering over Huffcutt and, picking up the rhetorical glove before him, declared, "I will say to the young man who has not lived long enough to know the facts in the case, that my words are true. If I am challenged, I will say that I, myself, have been at that hotel and seen it filled with drunken men and lewd women. A man could not take his family there without insult being offered to his wife and children. What I say here is true and there are men here who can be called to testify on their oath that it is true."

Huffcutt dropped his line of argument and went on to note that the park board was at the legal limit for the amount of debt it was allowed to acquire. Park board vice president Andrew C. Haugan made it clear that was no matter; a provision for payment would be made.

Two weeks later, the judiciary committee passed a substitute bill, accepting the commissioners' report and appropriating the money for the park. The acrimonious discussion had changed no one's mind. One nay voter was the cranky Senator Daniel Hixson, a member of the Farmers' Alliance from Grant County, Minnesota. He argued, "They got 52 acres, put brass buttons on it and called it the soldiers' home, and now they want the entire tract around the falls of Minnehaha. If the scheme goes the state will be called on to pay out millions of dollars for improvements. The whole thing is a fraud. They propose to build halls up there, for the display of flowers, and by and by they are going to have cinnamon bears on exhibition. I am opposed to the measure."[50]

Senator Charles S. Crandall from Owatonna read a letter from a widowed landowner at the falls (who could only have been Vinette) asking the senators to treat her and her family as they would have liked others to deal with their own when they could no longer protect them. Alas for her, no changes were made in the appraisals.

The appropriation bill passed the senate, went to the house, and passed there as well. A bill for Minneapolis to take over the parklands from the state (and maintain them or have them revert to the state) also passed. Unfortunately, there just wasn't enough money in the state treasury to pay for the park. Once again, it seemed as if the park would be lost.

It was George A. Brackett, of the state park commission and the Minneapolis park board, who solved the problem once and for all (of us). He began working on the solution in January 1889, when he convinced the park board, the Minneapolis legislative delegation, and Governor William R. Merriam to support the idea. His plan was to use private funds to secure the park, then have Minneapolis provide public money to repay those lenders. Brackett collected signatures on a note for $100,000. The signatories included Thomas Lowry (who owned the streetcar system), Dr. Samuel Hance, S. C. Gale, and A. J. Boardman (all of whom had invested in the land just west of the proposed park—and of course Boardman was a park board member, too), and a few others.[51]

Henry F. Brown (a real estate man who was partner to Charles Loring) had volunteered to guarantee the note; Brackett called on him. Brown simplified the process by providing $50,000 in cash and borrowing the rest. The check was cut and city council members handed it to the governor. The park bills were out of the legislature by the end of March 1889. The governor signed it. The park was finally secured.[52]

When George Lincoln died in the early 1880s, he left an estate of about $100,000. It was split between his wife and daughters: Vinette was given a third, and the rest was split among the three girls. George died too young, and Vinette must have been frightened at her prospects and the reduced status that came with losing her income. She needed the money she earned from renting her ground at the falls, and that income was taken from her. And her best recourse, she must have felt, was to made good on her promise to go the length of the law before she submitted to the loss of Minnehaha Falls.[53]

She launched another attack on the park board and this new park. She got a temporary injunction to prevent the state comptroller from repaying the park loan. She was playing both ends against the middle, claiming that the appraised value of her land was too low, but that receiving that amount would cause the assessed value of her other land in the area—and her taxes—to go up. It's a clever, constitutional claim, but she lost on her second hearing.

There was a minor irregularity in the way the park bill was approved and recorded in the legislature, and Vinette and her lawyers also tried out the theory that the park bill had never passed. While her suits against the legislature were in progress, Vinette also sued the park board. Samuel P. Cox, who had been working as a tourist photographer at the falls, took over the photography concession from the park board. He gave them an unthinkably large offer of $1,300 for the privilege for one year, and Vinette went to court to insist that she still had title to the land where the photographer's platform was perched, and that Cox should make payments on the concession to her.[54]

However, on June 7, 1889, Vinette Lincoln and her daughters Bertha, Florence, and Fanny gave up title to the park board, as did John Booth's heirs and a few other hopeful holdouts. With that, Minnehaha Park was firmly and forever established.[55]

5

The Sandman of Minnehaha Falls

I F ONE PERSON'S LIFE ENCAPSULATES the rowdyism and redemption of Minnehaha Falls, it is that of Robert Emil Fischer. He was a park policeman, a pavilion keeper, a park board member, a neighborhood resident, a maker of sand art souvenirs, and a racist. No matter how rampant the bad behavior around the falls got, or how vigorously people fought over the land there, Fischer was generally in the thick of it, and often on both sides. The story of Robert Fischer's life demonstrates the frantic scramble to exploit the falls, the interrelated families who supported each other's efforts, the dynamics between vendors and the city, and the wrenching transition between the era of private ownership and misbehavior at the falls to the generally placid park we know today—all stories that are addressed in later chapters.

Robert E. Fischer was born in Scott County, Minnesota, in 1859. His parents were German immigrants, and he had five, or perhaps seven, siblings. Over the years, his family became well acquainted with the Volks, another German family with their own six or eight children. In 1878, Robert's younger sister, Louisa, married one of the Volk sons, August. Louisa was fourteen and August was twenty-four. She was really young, and that's a big age gap. We might charitably think that children in nineteenth-century families married young so they could begin large families to help with the intense work required for survival. But whatever we might think, the Fischers and the Volks had no problem with it. That same year, the older Fischer daughter, Amelia, married another one of the Volk brothers named Jacob; they were both in their twenties.[1]

In 1881, some of the other boys in the Volk family moved to Minneapolis, taking work as stonemasons or carpenters. The next year,

Jacob found work as a cooper, and he and Amelia moved to the city, too. Robert Fischer followed soon after. At first, he enrolled at the University of Minnesota, beginning to study civil engineering, but he dropped out after a year and found various jobs doing railroad surveys and working in the flour mills.

Soon, August and Louisa followed their families to Minneapolis, where August took a job as a police officer and met Charlie R. Hill. Hill was then a former army man, and he had liked the soldier's life, having reenlisted multiple times. When he was in Helena, Montana, during a short period when he was not in the service, he had married a widow named Kate Hoffman, who had a little girl named Edith. The three of them eventually moved to Fort Snelling, where, of course, the more jovial side of life was right at his doorstep. Once Hill finished his last enlistment, the family moved to Minneapolis.

By 1883, Hill was on the police force and acquainted with August Volk. Three years later, Jacob Volk joined the force as well, and when surveying and flour milling didn't pan out, Robert Fischer became a Minneapolis city policeman, too.

With all of these connections between family and friends, it is perhaps unsurprising that Charlie Hill's stepdaughter Edith Hoffman married Robert Fischer. The wedding was held on New Year's Day in 1887 at Hill's house. Albert Alonzo Ames, then mayor of Minneapolis, was in attendance and signed the marriage certificate.

Everything seemed to be going well for Fischer. He was hired on to the mounted police force and took enormous pride in his position. He was known to ride up to a wedding and gallantly present the bride with a bouquet of flowers—an odd thing to do, but not without its charm. He and Edith moved to a home of their own, and eventually they had a son.

And then, in the summer of 1887, things fell apart.

Streetcar driver Thomas Tollefson was shot by thieves who were attempting to steal his cashbox. Brothers Tim and Pete Barrett were accused, and newspapers breathlessly covered the trial for weeks. Fischer knew the Barretts, who had, in fact, hung around Minnehaha for a while, committing armed robberies and frightening people. Fischer also knew they had committed the murder, but he withheld information about the crime from his superiors on the police force. Eventually, the Barretts were convicted and hanged. Fischer's connection to them was found out, and he was fired from the city's police force. Even his family's close relationship with Mayor Ames couldn't help him.[2]

All was not lost, however. Fischer's father-in-law, Charlie Hill, made his way up the ranks of the Minneapolis police department. At that time, the mayor's office handled the department's promotions, and because that mayor was Doc Ames, Hill easily advanced. He was promoted as high as colonel (Ames liked a military-styled police force), and in 1887, when the park board decided to form its own police force, he was selected as its first chief. From that new position, he could easily be a help to his son-in-law, and in 1888, Hill gave Fischer a new position on the park police force. Fischer might have been assigned

Charlie R. Hill, left, and Robert E. Fischer, right, in their park police uniforms, in Minnehaha Park, about 1890. *MNHS*

to the parkland at Bde Maka Ska; he moved near the east side of that lake the next year.

In 1889, after years of legal wrangling, the area around Minnehaha was finally wrested from the hands of private landowners and converted into Minnesota's first state park. The tourism businesses that had provided rowdy mayhem, fun, and snacks near the falls were torn down and removed from the new park. The park police were put in charge.

As part of the police presence, one of the patrolmen lived in the park in a house on Dutch Henry's former property, near today's Soldiers' Home bridge. Fischer and his wife lived there for three or four years, and this is where their daughter, Edith Minnehaha Fischer, was born. Hers is the first recorded birth in Minnehaha Park.[3]

In those days, policemen received no training. To do his job, Fischer used whatever on-the-job experience he had managed to get and whatever advice he could garner from those around him. He was the regular subject of complaints: he was rude, he was bossy, he was unpleasant to the public. In one instance, he and his partner, Frank Waltman, discovered some people who had gone behind the waterfall. When they ordered them out, the policemen made remarks about having to drive people like horned cattle, which, in those milder days of the 1890s, was taken as a terrible insult. The trespassers, incensed, brought the matter to the park board, which ruled that the officers should arrest people who refused to comply with the park rules, and they should also mind their language.[4]

FROM POLICEMAN TO MEDICINE MAKER

In 1890, some of the wealthy men who had bought up much of the land west of the park formed the Minnehaha Park Syndicate (discussed in detail below). Streets were laid out and the land was platted into blocks—perhaps four times the size of a city lot today—available for sale.

That same year, soon after he moved into the park policemen's house, Fischer bought one of those large lots to the west of the park for six hundred dollars. The man he bought it from had recently paid $118 for it. Fischer paid cash for the property, and before the year was out, he had purchased another lot that was about the same size.

This time, he took out a mortgage—but he paid it off in two days. For a slightly untrustworthy policeman with links to a shady mayor, this behavior raises a question: where did he get the money? At the time, Fischer made about sixty dollars a month on the force. He had managed to come up with more than three years' salary in cash, and there's no explanation for how he did it.

Robert and Edith moved out of the park policeman's house and into the home they built on their lot at the corner of East 49th Street and 37th Avenue. They would live there for the rest of their lives. Edith gave birth to four more daughters. The other girls eventually moved away, though Edith Minnehaha, the eldest daughter, named for the waterfall, lived just blocks away from the park for her entire life.

It was obvious to both the Fischers and the Volks that policing was not a stable profession. The wages weren't great, so perhaps it's not surprising that they augmented their income with a side business. Turning to their expertise in policing and masonry, some of the Volk brothers and Robert Fischer decided to incorporate the Volk Remedy Company and set themselves up as patent medicine manufacturers.

Patent medicine production was an ideal choice for slightly shady people. It was an industry involving poorly regulated curatives that preyed on people's fears and illnesses. In the late nineteenth century, patent medicine manufacturers took out patents and trademarks and then used marketing to vigorously promote their products and protect their intellectual property.

Though phrases like "quack" and "snake oil salesman" are still used to describe these proprietors of dubious nostrums, most people today have used products that were originally sold as patent medicines. These include brands like Bromo-Seltzer, Doan's Pills, and Vicks VapoRub. Lavoris mouthwash is Minneapolis's best-known patent medicine. These are all helpful concoctions, though of course not every patent medicine ended up being as helpful or effective.

We don't really know how effective the Volk Remedy Company's products were. Their top product—they only had two—was an ointment called Eureka Catarrhal Cure. Perhaps it worked. After all, no one complains about catarrh today. Fischer and the Volks got the recipe from a druggist named Hughes, who had a three-story drug-and-liquor store at Washington and Hennepin Avenues.

The Volks and Fischers, tradesmen and policemen, began their patent medicine careers. By 1895, their product was on offer at Donaldson's department store. That might have been the height of their success.

As time passed, the Volks relinquished their shares of the company to Robert Fischer. He ran the company, selling little tins of Eureka Catarrhal Cure by mail and in drugstores, until he died almost fifty years later. He eventually developed a second product as well—the reprehensibly named "Hindoo Oil," which supposedly cured everything from earaches to swollen feet and specifically promised it would not blister the skin. His family seemed to believe in these products. As his children grew up and moved away, they wrote letters home, asking for bottles and jars to be sent to themselves or to neighbors.

Ever the hustler, Fischer developed another side business as a perfume salesman, buying synthetic fragrances, creating blends, and selling them in minute vials.

All of these items sold for tiny amounts of money, and he had to work hard to even keep up with his paltry salary as a policeman. He knew he needed to do better. He knew he needed another line of work. And he found one at the falls, in its unexpected, free resource: colored sand.

To make a fortune, put sand in bottles

The Hughes Cut-Rate Drugstore was in a building that had previously housed the Minneapolis Dime Museum. That establishment had been a permanent sideshow of a place, featuring attractions like minstrel shows, human oddities ("See the Woman with the World's Largest Feet!"), or a two-headed calf (which was stuffed). Before landing in the building Hughes would later use, the Minneapolis Dime Museum was often in search of a new location or new proprietors. In March of 1889, another Dime Museum, in St. Paul, offered a show featuring Andrew Clemens of McGregor, Iowa, who was there to demonstrate his skills in filling bottles with sand.[5]

Clemens created designs inside bottles using colored sand that he got from Pictured Rocks, which is in Pikes Peak State Park near McGregor today. Using his own homemade tools, and arranging the sand in fancy bottles, sometimes grain by grain, he could spell out names, dates, and mottos and create detailed pictures of steamboats, flowers, and flags. The artistry is astounding. In 2021, one of his large bottles of sand sold for nearly a million dollars. Conveniently for Robert Fischer and others, colored sand is found abundantly at Minnehaha, too.

Around the same time that Clemens was performing at the Dime Museum, the legal battles over the ownership of Minnehaha Park were in their final throes. All that spring, the legislature was busy with bills and proposals to finally secure funding for the park. They filed the deed on June 15, 1889. That same day, the triumphant park superintendent William Berry, some park board members including A. J. Boardman, and the park police—likely including Robert Fischer—went down to the falls to clean house. All the businesses cluttering up the park were told to leave. The restaurants that sold picnic supplies, ice cream, or beer, the souvenir stands with bottles of colored sand, the person who took photographs of tourists in front of the waterfall: these people were leasing the land they were on, and that land now belonged to the park board. They all had a lot at stake, and most of them had very few resources.[6]

Given only thirty minutes' notice to vacate the new park, restaurant owner Harriet Collar refused to leave. She had come to the area with Egbert Collar, who leased the old Godfrey grist mill from 1883 until it burned down in about 1887. Harriet and Egbert don't appear to have actually been married. She was a widow and her surname was Eves, but she used Egbert's name while they lived together, probably because it was practical and would have been unseemly not to. She lived in the restaurant building with Egbert, his daughter Laura, and a small child known only as Babe. The park evictions put both her livelihood and her home at stake. Even worse, when the park board officials came to serve notice, Babe was terribly ill with stomach problems. When Harriet refused to leave, the men from the park board literally took the building down around her. The photographer she employed came at them with a gun, but he eventually surrendered to the police. Babe's ailment got worse, and she died at Minnehaha Falls three days after the eviction.

Harriet Collar had no time to mourn. She had to find a home and an income. She had sold souvenirs—both photographs of the falls and bottles of colored sand—at her restaurant. As soon as she secured a new place to live, she rented a display space at St. Anthony Falls to sell sand art and photographs.

Harriet Collar's pavilion, as seen about 1888 from the lip of the falls, with the Soldiers' Home buildings against the sky. Barnet's pavilion occupied the same space in 1903 and 1904.

After the great tragedy and loss at the falls, Egbert Collar wandered off someplace far beyond the edges of this story. He left his daughter Laura behind with Harriet, who soon took up with the photographer who provided the pictures she sold. His name was Luther Melvin Hyde, but absolutely everyone called him L. Mel. He had been in Minneapolis for decades. He also made those souvenirs from the colored sands at Minnehaha Falls. When Andrew Clemens demonstrated his amazing skills at the Dime Museum, L. Mel was no doubt in the audience.[7]

There are no known examples of L. Mel's sand art today. But he taught the craft to Robert Fischer, who made sand art for the rest of his life, and some of Fischer's sand art survives. Years later, we find this write-up of Fischer's technique:

It is delicate and painstaking work. Using a series of different sized tubes and quills, he pours in sand of every color—red, blue, white, green, brown, purple, yellow—and arranges it in lines, ridges, circles and blocks which show through the glass. This takes time, patience and an almost uncanny skill. Once the sand is in place it cannot be moved or rearranged—and a single jar will ruin the entire design.

After watching him work for an hour or more, it is still impossible to tell just how he achieves his results. But achieve that he does, working out designs resembling Indian beadwork, pictures of animals, birds and people, and artistic studies of mountains, trees, rivers, lakes and waterfalls.[8]

Robert Fischer's sand art, 2019. *HHM*

Fischer estimated that he made over forty-five thousand sand pictures in glass bottles over his lifetime. It became a significant business for him. He moved on to making sand art pictures of Yellowstone and Glacier National Parks, using sand from those locations. He even made sand art featuring Hibbing on Minnesota's Iron Range.

Like some other proprietors who were forced out, L. Mel Hyde and Harriet Eves (Collar) eventually moved to a strip of land at the park's northern edge. Harriet set herself up in a new business that surely no one could object to—growing sweet peas—and she became quite successful. During the season, she, Laura, and L. Mel could pick eight thousand blossoms a day and sell them to the big department stores downtown. She might have continued in this fragrant venture for a long time, but the park board bought that strip of land—the Godfrey Tract, or the 200-Foot Strip—out from under her in 1903, thereby destroying her home and her livelihood a second time.[9]

Harriet, L. Mel, and Laura picked up and moved to Oregon. L. Mel sold all of his photographic equipment, a large stock of photographs, and his sand art supplies to Robert Fischer.

THE TROUBLES WITH THE PARK POLICE

Robert Fischer left the park police force after five years. He was not rehired in 1893, probably due to the complaints that had been filed against him. It seems he found it hard to give up policing, however, and he retained his uniform and wore it daily at the park. His old partner, Frank Waltman, had moved into the park policeman's house on the old Dutch Henry property. Waltman didn't get in the way of Fischer "playing cop." Quite possibly, the two men had worked together to run a bunco operation; quite possibly that is where the money came from to buy the land near the park where Fischer built his house.

In 1896, Waltman was called before a park board committee, where he was "allowed the privilege of explaining away certain charges." Whatever was said (and it was not recorded), Waltman was fired and told to vacate the house. He returned home to pack up, but then he killed himself with a gun. About ten days later, the park board objected to an implication that Fischer was a park policeman. "They say that Fisher [sic] has not been so employed for three years past. When he left the force, he retained his uniform and has been wearing it daily, which might lead to the impression that he was still an officer."[10]

By 1897, Fischer had finally given up both policing unseemly behavior and his own unseemly policing behavior. The Volk Remedy Company, his perfume business, and the sand art brought in some money, but not enough to provide for his growing family. Fischer switched sides and opened his own refreshment pavilion just north of 50th Street and Hiawatha Avenue.

The Fischer pavilion was on the strip of land known by then as Runyan's Addition, west of the park along Hiawatha Avenue. While Harriet and L. Mel had set up their sweet pea operation on the north edge of the park, others like Fischer organized the park's west edge to supply the wants of tourists, visitors, and merrymakers. Once these new establishments went up, a couple of plainclothes police dropped by for a visit. After discovering free-flowing illegal alcohol sales, they got warrants, returned with the Third Precinct's paddy wagon, and started making arrests. Six people went to jail. Though Fischer ran a seemingly straightforward business (and there were several similar pavilions in the area with good-enough reputations), he was one of those arrested. He paid a fine of seventy-five dollars for selling alcohol without a license.[11]

At his pavilion, Fischer sold ice cream, candy, and souvenirs, which included his sand art bottles and photos of Minnehaha Falls. The days of tourists posing for professional photographers with the waterfall as background ended in about 1890; now, Fischer just sold the same few photos of the waterfall again and again, reprinting them as necessary from L. Mel's original glass plates. He eventually subleased the pavilion to someone else, but he likely continued to supply the place with wares for sale. By the early 1900s, his lease on the land under the pavilion had run out, and a house mover bought the pavilion for just five dollars.[12]

TO MAKE THE WORLD THE WAY YOU WANT IT, RUN FOR OFFICE

The events around Fischer's pavilion that took place during the years of raucous behavior are described in the chapters that follow. But in the last years of his life, Fischer began yet another career. He got involved with local Democratic politics, though he wasn't welcomed into the party. He was rumored to be a mugwump, one who had switched sides. That's a bit of an unfair criticism, as switching parties was not an unfamiliar tactic at the time. (Mayor Ames, for example, switched parties whenever it was convenient. And even A. J. Boardman, the real estate man and park board member who had aided in the demolition of Harriet Collar's house, switched from Republican to Democrat when he was considering a run for mayor.) The Democratic party in Minneapolis's Twelfth Ward was led by Sylvanus A. Stockwell, a committed and principled liberal who walked up to the edge of, but never crossed over into, socialism. Fischer didn't fit in with the principled liberal crowd. Neither did he fit in with the Socialists, who were rabble-rousing throughout the body politic—and some of whom would soon set up the rowdiest dance hall the falls would ever see. He didn't fit in with the respectable Republicans, either, who were organized against businesses like his. Fischer was too warily middle-of-the-road for either side, and he found himself an outcast among the Twelfth Ward Democrats in the neighborhood around the falls.

Still, Fischer ran for office several times. In 1902, he came in fourth of five candidates in the Democratic primary for alderman. He campaigned on the idea of extending the electric streetcar to Fort Snelling, but it was a Republican landslide year; he stood no chance. He ran for the park board in 1906 and again in 1912, no doubt in response to the board's disastrous decision to fence off the neighborhoods to the west of the park from accessing the streetcars on Minnehaha Avenue. That move (described in Chapter 8) had been meant to appease the park's more upstanding neighbors, who were worried—even at that late date—that rowdyism was still liable to break free and overrun the park again. Fischer also attempted a run for the state legislature, but he failed there, too.[13]

He was eventually elected to the park board in 1915, and he immediately had his teenaged daughter Edith petition the committee on privileges for the right to make and sell sand art souvenirs in the park. The privileges committee's vote split, and the president then called for a full board vote. The board defeated the proposal in a seven-to-five vote. The president remarked, "It would establish a very bad

Robert Fischer's campaign card, 1902. He came in fourth of five candidates in the primary election.

ROBERT E. FISCHER,

Candidate for Democratic Nomination for
ALDERMAN OF TWELFTH WARD.

Born in Minnesota in 1859; came to Minneapolis from a Farm in 1878. Worked at common labor, railroading and in flour mills, also on government and railroad surveys Resident of what is now the 12th Ward for twenty years. Has five children born in this Ward, Is now and for the past 10 years engaged in the proprietory medicine business. Has not heretofore sought an elective office. He is not controlled by any "clique" or "ring" either in or out of politics. Residence, 37th Ave. and E. 49th St.

No Primary Election except Sept. 16 the first Registration Day. Polls open from 6 a. m. to 9 p. m. You can vote the ticket of but one Political Party at the primary election. 2nd Registration day, Tuesday Oct. 21st. 3d Registration day, Saturday, Oct. 25th. General election, Nov. 4th, 1902.

OVER.

precedent." Unsurprisingly, Fischer voted for his daughter's proposal; after all, nepotism had worked well for him in the past, so why not try it again? His daughter, of course, was not the actual sand artist making the proposal. Whether the park board knew it or not, putting her name on the request was just a way for Fischer to get around the board's inclinations.[14]

After serving four and a half years, he resigned his park board seat in 1919. The *Minneapolis Tribune* report was distinctly catty about it: "Mr. Fischer explained that his holding of a city office prevented him from doing business with the city, and he felt that he should resign rather than let his business interests suffer longer. Mr. Fischer is a medicine manufacturer."[15]

A PRODUCT OF HIS OWN HARD TIMES

From the time he was a young man, Robert Fischer was found at Minnehaha Park. He knew the park through official channels and shady ones, as a friend to some confectioners, and as someone who often looked the other way. Like many of the characters at the park, Fischer was just shifty enough to get by somehow and just honest enough to keep trying to do things right. He tried to inhabit the middle of the road in many ways, and he never truly succeeded. No one who attempted to get rich from Minnehaha ever did so—not even Franklin Steele; it was a tiny part of his operation. But the affection people had, and have, for the place meant more than making a killing. People like Fischer who lived in the neighborhood never left. And his opinions about that neighborhood can be read from his creations, his public service, and his willingness to work to keep his family going. His opinions can also be deduced from the things he left behind.

There were whispers among Fischer's family that he was a member of the Ku Klux Klan, though this is not known for sure. His views about race are not in doubt, however. Postcards in his estate carry demeaning stereotypes; these were mementos he had saved for decades. Fischer tried, in his tiny way, to profit off the conflict over Prohibition, which was ratified the year he left the park board. He created a souvenir postcard, a strange, ugly object made of two cards glued together. On one side two men are filling a jug, and on the other side, they tip the jug up to drink. The jug is represented by some sort of clear plastic layers; within the layers is sand from Minnehaha. It's a wet/dry joke, where nothing but sand pours from cask or bottle. The postcard Fischer invented gives us a glimpse into his creativity but also into the darker, angrier subtleties of his personality. The drinkers were African Americans, depicted in grotesquely racist cartoon drawings. It is the most distinctly revealing item Fischer left behind.

6

Morally Questionable People
Having Fun

W HEN MINNEHAHA PARK WAS ESTABLISHED IN 1889, a slowly
escalating conflict began at the falls. The neighborhood around
the park grew quickly. The real estate developers, pavilion owners, and
new neighbors had interests that sometimes intersected but mostly
clashed. For the next thirteen years, until "war" was declared in 1902,
tensions slowly escalated, as misbehavior, disputes, and enforcement
of the law continued to disturb the peace at the falls. Though the park
board had control of their land—Minnehaha Park—they were drawn
into the strife on their borders.

The park board understood from the beginning how well loved
and heavily visited Minnehaha Park would be. They took seriously
their custodianship of this lovely laughing waterfall and the grounds
around it. They knew that the public expected hospitality there.

Soon after they took ownership of Minnehaha Park in 1889, and
after they chased out all the people living—and making a living—
within the new park's boundaries, the park board invested in the
area in ways that they thought important, but also that they could
afford. They added picnic tables and hammocks. They graded gravel
walking paths, planted flower beds that spelled out "Minnehaha Park
Pride of Minneapolis," and grew grass on what had been completely
bare ground. The new electric streetcar line, added to Minnehaha
Avenue in 1891, replaced the motor line and improved access for city
residents.[1]

In 1892 the board built the picnic pavilion, which was designed
by prominent Minneapolis architect and park board member Harry

Wild Jones. Erected among the trees to the northeast of where the refectory stands today, the pavilion provided every convenience for the free use of visitors in preparing meals: tables, stove, and cooking utensils. Plans called for the building to cost between $3,000 and $5,000.

> This new pavilion will cover a ground space of 52 × 87 feet. It will have only one floor, which will be entirely clear for dancing purposes, except around the outside where six feet away from the balustrade a row of posts will hold up the roof. At one end there will be two rooms, one a waiting room 20 feet square with a large open fire-place and mantel of red pressed brick, and adjoining this is another room 20 feet square where a kitchen range will be located for the convenience of those wishing to heat water for coffee. On the outside of the balustrade a broad seat will be placed, having a back of turned balusters.
>
> The principal construction will be of Georgia pine, finished in natural wood; the roof will be shingled with red cedar shingles, with copper cresting, finials, and flashings. The general appearance of the building will be something similar to that of the Lake Harriet pavilion, except that being one story in height it will appear lower and the large roof will suggest protection and shelter from the weather, which in fact will be its main purpose.[2]

This picnic pavilion gave groups a place for their church picnics and dances. It added to the options for hospitable gatherings at the falls but wasn't an income source for the park board, as they paid someone to be in charge of the place.

THE MINNEHAHA PARK SYNDICATE

As the park board began providing amenities, the people who had been investing in the land around the park were also promoting the area. Their efforts had started some years earlier. In 1883, a millwright named Edward M. Runyan decided to try his hand at real estate and

The park board brought family-friendly amenities to Minnehaha. The board began accepting donated animals for a zoo in 1893, the same year a vendor began offering pony rides in the park. One of the few reminders of the zoo is the name for a section of the park: the Deer Pen. In this area, once surrounded by a high fence, the board kept bison, deer, elk, and sometimes even a moose. At the top western edge of the Deer Pen, the zoo housed an array of animals, everything from guinea pigs to bears, even the cinnamon bears that state Senator Daniel Hixson had been so threatened by back in 1889. The zoo was shut down when Theodore Wirth took over as superintendent in 1906; many of the animals were in bad health, having been very poorly cared for. Some had to be put down. Others were transferred in 1907 to the Longfellow Gardens Zoo across Hiawatha Avenue from Minnehaha Park. But the hoofed stock stayed in the Deer Pen until 1923.

The pens and cages that once housed the other zoo animals are long gone, but a careful eye can find their footings by looking below the top western edge of the Deer Pen in early spring, before the leaves come out.[vi]

Bears and visitors at the Minnehaha zoo, about 1899

formed the North Star Real Estate Company. He had a great break late in the year, when he got the exclusive sales rights to Palmer's Addition to Minneapolis. This was a large tract lying between Minnehaha Avenue and what became Hiawatha Avenue, from about 34th Street South to 41st Street. It was platted into lots to be sold and added to the city. Minneapolis was growing south. Minnehaha Avenue, constructed in the 1870s, ran from the city straight to the falls; it paralleled the Milwaukee Road train tracks. With roads and railroad access, this part of the city was opening up. Runyan was there to take advantage of it.

By June 1885, Ed Runyan's real estate company was offering lots in the Minnehaha Park addition. These half-acre lots were due west of the "proposed state park" between today's Minnehaha Parkway on the north and 50th Street on the south, and between 34th and 38th Avenues. The next year, Runyan was selling land a bit west of that Minnehaha Park Addition. The new parcel, Lake Amelia Outlots, was at the northeast corner of Lake Nokomis.

In 1887, Runyan helped form the Minnehaha Improvement Association. Over the years, several groups seem to have used this name. The members of this version of the Improvement Association were in real estate, and they included Ed Runyan, Dr. Samuel Hance, and park board commissioner Albert J. Boardman (who was in real estate with his brother William). Boardman Street, south and west of the falls, is named for Albert and William Boardman, and it bisects the land they wanted to increase in value: Boardman's State Park Addition to Minneapolis. The association existed to increase the value of the land they owned between the proposed park at Minnehaha Falls and Lake Nokomis.

One of their first actions was to extract promises from the management of the Milwaukee Road for a fifteen-cent round-trip fare between the Minnehaha depot and the city. Such a low fare was affordable to nearly all, and it would encourage home-building. The association planted trees along 50th Street between Lake Nokomis (then called Lake Amelia) and Minnehaha Falls and eventually donated land between lake and waterfall for the road we know as East Minnehaha Parkway today. They also sold lots in a housing district along that parkway that included, according to the *St. Paul Globe,* "other restrictive measures (besides the requirement that all buildings must cost at least $1,500)"; "in this way the vicinity is to be made very desirable."[3]

Ed Runyan moved his office from the city out to Minnehaha in 1888. He kept a lot for himself and built a house at the corner of 39th Avenue and 49th Street. The exact way that he met Vinette Lincoln has been lost to time, but some of the details of this important connection are available. Vinette lost the land within Minnehaha Park in 1889 and collected her payment for it. She and her daughters still owned a good-sized parcel on the west side of Hiawatha Avenue, and she had it surveyed in May 1890, about a year after the park-related legal battle. This was platted into large lots, and the whole parcel was renamed "Geo. W. Lincoln's Addition to Minnehaha Park" in December 1890. The timing on this matches up with the city council's efforts to open Hiawatha Avenue, which parallels Minnehaha Avenue from the city out to 54th Street. ("Opening the road" was a formal process whereby the city described and mapped the edges of the road, then took it over as a city street. The landowners generally got no payment for their land, because the loss to them was considered offset by the benefit of having a road to their property.)[4]

With increased access to this part of town that included Minnehaha Park, and Vinette's ongoing need for cash, she had begun selling land; what she sold and what she held had major consequences for commercial activity at the falls.

The most important land that Vinette and her daughters owned was the land closest to the park. This land is today entirely occupied by MN-55 (Hiawatha Avenue) and the twentieth-century light-rail tracks. In the way of things at Minnehaha, some of this was sold and re-bought by the Lincolns. Some of it was sold outright, some was foreclosed on, and ultimately, this part of the Lincoln Addition was replatted into Runyan's Addition, with more than thirty little lots facing the park. To the end, Vinette and her daughters kept lots 3–11 in Runyan's Addition.

At the same time as Hiawatha Avenue was opened and as the Lincoln Addition was platted, Runyan's two organizations, the North Star Real Estate Company and the Minnehaha Improvement Association— neither of which had been heard from for a bit—were replaced by the Minnehaha Park Syndicate. This was a far more high-powered group, incorporated with $400,000 in capital. Dr. Samuel Hance and Ed

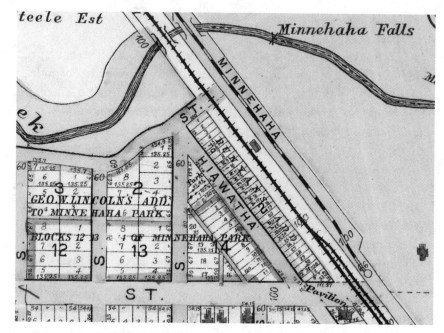

This 1892 detail of Runyan's Addition shows lots 3-11 opposite the railroad depot, where the Gardners would establish the Minnehaha Midway. In the lower right is Foster's Pavilion; in the park is the park policeman's house. *C. M. Foote and Co., City of Minneapolis, University of Minnesota Libraries, detail*

Runyan were both members, and so was the former mayor George Pillsbury; Llewellyn Christian, part owner of the Crown Roller Mill and one of the Christian family who made fortunes in milling flour; Richard J. Mendenhall, banker, greenhouse owner, enslaver; and another banker named A. Frank Gale. Runyan's Addition was platted and accepted by the city council in 1891, at the same time that the council accepted plats for Pillsbury's Addition and for Mendenhall's Addition, both just west of the falls. The new electric streetcar line, opened that year, could deliver residents to jobs downtown. The Minnehaha Park Syndicate was ready to shepherd the growth of this residential district. And they surely expected to make some money along the way.[5]

The area was fairly quiet, too. It seemed a safe bet that whatever was going on at the falls was a minor disturbance in the staid and growing neighborhood west of the park. The Methodists were planning a new church nearby. Lots were selling. Houses began to go up. But Vinette Lincoln was not yet done with her land, nor, seemingly, with messing with the park board. She rented lots 3–11 of Runyan's Addition to refreshment vendors. In a few years, it would become known as the Minnehaha Midway.

CHARACTERS LACKING CHARACTER

Both before and after creation of Minnehaha as a park, details of the unseemly antics at the falls are hard to uncover. Newspaper stories reacted to, or alluded to, the ongoing mischief; they hardly ever described it directly. It's much the same with old photographs. Finding any nineteenth-century photograph of someone in a sloppy or lewd drunken posture is pretty rare, and when one limits the search to 125 acres in the southeast corner of Hennepin County, the search is unlikely to the point of impossible.[6]

While the picnic pavilion seems to have been a popular public building, it happens that the people running it were probably shady, or at least supportive of merriment and fun. This becomes evident in tracing a web of connections. In 1897, the care of the pavilion was given to Harriet Reeves, a widow whose husband, William, had passed away a few years before. William was a Civil War vet and a member of the GAR's George N. Morgan Post. A former policeman, he had held patronage jobs like county jailor. The Reeves were acquaintances of one Evert Nymanover, described by every newspaper in town as a "fawn-eyed socialist." These connections with the Morgan post, the Minneapolis police, and the socialist movement were shared by Adelbert Gardner and his son, Irwin. And by the mid-1890s the Gardners, father and son, would turn up the flames of intemperate and raunchy behavior at the outer edges of Minnehaha Park. Though Harriet Reeves was a paid park board employee, she could surely be counted on not to interfere with the refreshment vendors across Minnehaha Avenue. And before long, she left her place as keeper of the picnic pavilion. The job went to a man named Burke O'Brien.[7]

Burke O'Brien was the black sheep of an otherwise respectable family of early settlers. His brother Frank wrote a pretty good Minnesota history in 1904. That history left out Burke's years as a city alderman, where he was, according to the *Journal* (Minneapolis's more liberal newspaper), "a soft mark for friends with personal interests to serve." When Burke went on to join the Minneapolis police force, he used his position to aid criminal enterprise. He was convicted for alerting the managers of a gambling house that a warrant had been issued for their arrest. Yet the park board still allowed him to run the picnic pavilion at a time when the newspaper described him as "wholly unfit for any position of public responsibility."[8]

Dubious respectability was the one certainty among the characters at Minnehaha.

The confectioners and other small businesses that had been ejected from park property in 1889 continued to serve visitors. Some proprie-

What is a confectionery?

The businesses just outside Minnehaha Park were most commonly known as confectioneries. Although this isn't a term we use today, we still have the idea: the gas station mini-mart that sells candy, soda pop, and cigarettes is the confectionery of our era.

We can learn a great deal about a confectionary business in the 1890s from an inventory of furnishings that Robert E. Fischer prepared in 1898. His confectionery stand, just west of Minnehaha Park at the corner of 50th Street, operated from 1897 to 1901; in 2018, his family still held his business records and examples of his wares. He listed:

wall case and shelving	2 tubular lanterns
2 counters	30 glasses
3 showcases	20 ice cream dishes
1 ice box	20 spoons
3 brass lamps	1 corn popper
8 tables	2 gasoline torches
26 chairs	1 ice plane
1 scale	1 tub
14 candy jars	3 buckets
20 candy trays	3 pictures

His confectionary offered candy and popcorn, ice cream, cold drinks, and a place to sit down. There were no electric lights in this part of Minneapolis in the 1890s, and so Fischer provided lantern light and torch light for his evening customers. He filled his display cases with Minnehaha Falls souvenirs to sell to visitors, including Harriet Collar's and L. Mel Hyde's photographs of the falls, and he sold his own colorful handmade Minnehaha sand art souvenirs.[vii]

tors, like Harriet Eves (Collar) and Samuel P. Cox, changed careers. Other owners set themselves up in locations on the north and west edges of the park boundaries. Some of them had noteworthy or lasting impacts on the history of Minnehaha Park. In trying to make as much money as possible, a few ran shady, troublesome businesses that eventually caused outrage among the neighbors.

In 1891 longtime settler and local postmaster Andrew J. Foster built a refreshment pavilion on land he owned just outside the park, at the corner of East 50th Street and Hiawatha Avenue. Today the 50th Street light-rail train stop is on this site. Foster strategically placed his new business at the end of the new electric streetcar line. The *Tribune* carried his advertisements for "beautiful souvenirs," coffee, and sandwiches made from "Ivey's cream bread." Though one could get a drink of illegal alcohol there, Foster's confectionary was a generally respectable place.[9]

William Poudler built a refreshment stand just south of East 49th Street along Minnehaha Avenue. He had fallen in love with a woman named Isabel, and after they married, he left his career as a well digger and set the two of them up in the business she liked, running a refreshment stand at Minnehaha Falls. It was originally a modest place, just twelve by twelve feet, but in it Poudler became the longest-standing of the confectioners: he stayed in business right outside Minnehaha Park nearly until the end of his life in the 1920s. Poudler, like Foster, was a generally respected and respectable businessman.[10]

Other confectioners operated during this period of the 1890s, and not all of them were respectable or family-friendly. The first exception was Sidney C. Babcock.

SOLDIERS FROM THE FORT, UNESCORTED WOMEN, AND A LIVELY SOCIAL SCENE

Sidney Babcock was a millwright by training who had married a woman twenty years younger than himself. They had a large family, and they originally opened a confectionery and grocery at 3002 Minnehaha Avenue. Babcock expanded this confectionery business to his stand at the falls, on land just west of the old Steele-Lincoln house. His little candy and pop stand did not last long in that location outside the park. He said that the "parties running the establishment in the

Lincoln house rented the ground from under him, to get rid of his competition." (Who those "parties" were and what they were up to in the Steele-Lincoln house remains a mystery.)[11]

Forced to move, Babcock found a new spot closer to Fort Snelling, where he built a pavilion and a dance hall. This was somewhere just outside the park, west of the railroad tracks and a few hundred yards south of the Milwaukee depot. It was between Foster's pavilion and the former site of Dutch Henry's rowdy dance hall. In October 1892, the *Minneapolis Tribune* described the situation that Babcock was moving into. The soldiers from the fort were known to go to Minnehaha Falls—especially on Sundays—and "run things to suit their own ideas." Under the headline "Boors from the Fort," the *Tribune* said that several of the soldiers seemed to be spoiling for a fight, and "They were hardly as gentlemanly and polite as men in their station are popularly supposed to be. They are quite the reverse, according to reports of police officers and others who spend quite a bit of time at Minnehaha Park and vicinity. Unescorted women get more attention than they bargained for. A pretty woman is looked upon as the proper party for a 'mash.'"[12]

The slang term "masher" has fallen from our vocabulary, but the type is unfortunately instantly recognizable. A man who makes aggressive sexual overtures to women he does not know used to be called a masher.

At this time in 1892, Officer Robert E. Fischer was the park policeman living in Minnehaha Park. He arrested at least one soldier for disorderly conduct. Private George Bergeron from Company H, Third Infantry, was sentenced to pay ten dollars or spend ten days in the workhouse. His commanding officer was reportedly quite annoyed at the park police, and not at his soldier.

This sort of aggressive rowdyism was not welcomed by the neighborhood's new residents, those upstanding citizens who were busily buying lots from the Minnehaha Park Syndicate and building their country homes. Slowly, over the next year or two, Babcock's became a place where the soldiers congregated, and so did the young ladies, mashers or no. The young men of the city followed the women. Young people indulged in a lively social scene. There was not enough reprehensible behavior to make the papers, so perhaps Babcock managed to put a little restraint on the crowds. Whatever restraint might have been exercised, it did not last.

ADELBERT GARDNER APPEARS ON THE SCENE

Back in 1886, on Christmas night, two hundred socialists with their working-class families gathered in Martin's Hall on the corner of Washington and Cedar Avenues, in an immigrant neighborhood about a mile from downtown Minneapolis. After speeches in English, German, and Swedish, the children were all given candy and dancing commenced, continuing until 4 AM: "La Marseillaise was sung at midnight in chorus by the whole house." A newcomer named Adelbert L. Gardner led the speeches.[13]

Within a few years, Adelbert Gardner and his son, Irwin, would be running a dance hall at the falls, and they would become the instigators of the Minnehaha Midway. In the final era of rowdyism, they were the chief perpetrators of the illegal and immoral behavior at the falls that so shocked and upset the citizens of Minneapolis.

Adelbert Gardner was born in 1849 in Brookfield, a small town in upstate New York. He was a middle child in a large family. His father died when he was small, and he spent part of his youth farmed out to neighbors, likely because they could feed him. In early 1865, he made his way to Schenectady, a hundred miles from home, where on January 27, he joined the Union Army. Although he signed up for a three-year tour, he was discharged on May 24 of that same year in Washington, DC. The Civil War was over. But Adelbert had been sick in the hospital since February 28, and while he could possibly have had a month of service in the field, he probably saw no action. His discharge papers say that his eyes were blue, that his hair and complexion were light, and that he was five foot, three and a half inches tall. They don't mention that he was only fifteen years old. He was back home in a few weeks.

Years later, he was known around Minneapolis as a Union veteran and a Grand Army man. He sounded reveille at GAR encampments and played the fife in the fife and drum corps at a GAR post. Perhaps he admitted to his short four months of service; perhaps he didn't.

In 1889, Adelbert Gardner was an increasingly prominent political organizer who had switched affiliation from the socialists to the Farmers' Alliance, a significant political party in Minnesota and in the Midwest. By the end of the year, Gardner was the alliance's deputy state lecturer for Minnesota's first congressional district, and he was living in Mower County. There was every sign that a successful political career was in the offing.

It is not clear if Adelbert Gardner was a fiery speaker, a brilliant organizer, a glad-handing schmoozer, or all of these. Whatever his skills and personality, in 1890, a faction of the Farmers' Alliance turned against him. He was accused of several sorts of malfeasance: an insurance scam, attempting to vote without credentials at the state convention, not actually being a farmer. The Farmers' Alliance published a weekly newspaper, *The Great West,* and its editor clearly hated Gardner, calling him a "sneak" and a "deceptive genius." He continued briefly as the district lecturer, then left his job and returned to the Twin Cities.[14]

Though still working in politics, he became a hotelkeeper, running a working-class boardinghouse called the Hotel Gardner on the corner of University and Cleveland Avenues in St. Paul, just by the railroad tracks that still cross that area today. The Gardner family lived there in 1894 and 1895, even through a disastrous kitchen fire. With around-the-clock noise from the rail yards and the manure smell and flies from stockyards just a few hundred yards away, it can't have been pleasant.

The Gardners needed to improve their fortunes. Adelbert Gardner used his connections and his ability to draw a crowd and turned to a new opportunity: the refreshment pavilion business at beautiful Minnehaha Falls.

"Rollicking fun"

In the summer of 1895, the social scene at Minnehaha went from an indecorous simmer to a licentious, rolling boil. Adelbert Gardner had arrived. Just as happened with his brief and tempestuous career organizing within the Farmers' Alliance, in a very short time he was at the center of a controversy.

The story—told as a long exposé on promiscuity and wild behavior at the dance halls at the falls—made the front page of the *Minneapolis Tribune* on August 6, 1895. Gardner had linked up with a married couple, Louis and Sophia Cass, who lived in their refreshment pavilion, built on a lot on Minnehaha Avenue that they leased from Vinette Lincoln. Gardner built a dance hall right next to their confectionary stand, and they split the proceeds from these businesses.

Gardner turned up the dial on creating a sideshow atmosphere. He hired an organ grinder to wheeze out tired, tinkling music, and maybe there was a monkey to beg peanuts or coins from passersby. Gardner also gave free rein to the racial hatred known at the falls and made memorable by Dutch Henry's minstrel shows. Gardner set up the carnival "game" called the African Dodger. It was simple enough: try to hurt or kill that man to win a cigar. The weapon was a baseball, thrown from enough distance that maybe the man had a chance to not get hit. A Black man (or a white man in blackface) stood behind a piece of canvas that had a hole cut in it, and he put his head through the hole. On the attacker's side, the canvas was painted to look like a slave cabin with an open door and the body of a man standing in the doorway. When the man stuck his head through the hole, he became a live target. If the dodger was fast enough, he could pull his head out of the hole before taking a baseball in the face. But he couldn't control who chose to play. Consider that, at Minnehaha Falls, a professional baseball player (Elmer Foster, son of Andrew Foster, pavilion keeper at 50th and Hiawatha) lived just a block from this setup, and he would have walked past it to reach the train or streetcar tracks. This horrible activity was once common at carnivals.[15]

Cass and Gardner acquired a piano, hired some fiddle players and a dance caller, and began advertising dances at the falls. They started with two days a week, but soon were having dances on Tuesday, Wednesday, Thursday, and Saturday. While Sophia and Louis Cass ran the confectionery side, Adelbert Gardner himself worked the crowd to fill the dance floor with couples, all paying their nickels to dance quadrilles and waltzes. He would walk a man up to a single girl, ask her name, and introduce them. "So matter-of-fact was he that the girls seemed to have no volition except to dance with the men the little fellow brought them," explained the *Tribune*. It was important to fill the dance floor, not just to make money but because quadrilles—a sort of square dance—require a set number of dancers. And women were forbidden to dance together, probably because it was bad for business.

The chief scandal of these dance halls was that unescorted young women went there to consort with Fort Snelling's soldiers and the young men of the city. While newspaper editors had an opinion about how much attention an unescorted woman might want, the women had their own ideas. The streetcars were simply "loaded with women." Some of them were factory girls who lived at home. Dressed in their Gibson Girl shirtwaists and long skirts, and wearing stylish black sailor hats with little veils, these young women were anticipating "rollicking fun" at the falls. And to the annoyance of

The exposé printed in the Minneapolis Tribune *on August 6, 1895, paid particular attention to the actions of young women.*

The dances . . . begin about dusk, but they are not in full glory until it is about the hour when most people go to bed. On almost any of these nights, all the way from 8 to 10 o'clock, the cars running to Minnehaha are loaded with women. The curious fact is that there seem to be two women to every man, most of the girls going to these dances without an escort. Some of these women act with the greatest of freedom on the cars, so much so that ladies living at the falls are very much annoyed. . . . A week ago a number of civilians, largely men from the Minnehaha Driving Park, decided to drive out the soldiers and have the girls to themselves. There were fully 30 of the civilians and about half as many soldiers. A fight followed and the soldiers retreated in disorder. It is claimed that this has created a fierce feud between the bluecoats and the civilians, which will be fought to a finish when the first opportunity occurs. The soldiers have had peaceable possession of the places; in fact, they were started largely for their benefit, and maintained by their patronage, and every sense of fairness is in favor of the soldiers. The opposition is largely a feeling of jealousy, as the brass buttons are great favorites with the ladies everywhere. . . .

After the quadrille many of the dancers went outside. A number started for the lonely walks around the falls, and others went down the tracks to the other dancing establishment. The railroad track became, in fact, a regular promenade. Couples would form in one pavilion and go out for a walk and soon appear at the other. . . . Soldiers were having a nice time with the girls. They did not seem to care to go into the pavilions as long as they had such company outside. Up and down they walked with their arms around their sweethearts, their caresses returned in full measure.

The question that presented itself most forcefully to the ignorant observer was where all the men and women went during the recesses between the quadrilles. For a few minutes there might be almost no women in sight, then when Pat, or the caller at the Babcock establishment was ready to announce another quadrille, back they would troop from the walks and the railroad track for another whirl.

So the giddy dance kept up until the last car.

the "well-bred, self-respecting" ladies who lived in the newly built houses near the park, these women visiting the dance halls were not so constrained by Victorian virtue. The conflict seems too gentle to be real to us today, though the words used to describe each group are still with us: "Strait-laced" or "loose." "Puritanical or "permissive." "Conservative" or "liberal." Some of the women who frequented the pavilions were prostitutes, "the women who go to the falls on business." But most of them were independent wage earners with their own money to spend. Probably many were looking for a husband as well as a good time. People in higher social classes met their spouses by acquaintanceship and personal introduction; the women at the dance halls put a price on society's vision of their moral integrity: a five-cent dance with men they didn't know.

And so continued the summer of 1895. Early August was as pleasant as it comes, not too hot in the bright dry days and cooling at night, the season past the worst of the mosquitoes as the sun set. People flocked to this new arrangement, dancing at Babcock's or Gardner's pavilion and strolling in couples between the two. Many of those strollers wandered over to see the waterfall, or ducked into quiet dark areas of the park to be alone. In the dark, the chirping of the crickets hailed the approaching autumn. The dance hall patrons took full advantage of what Babcock, Cass, and Gardner offered: license to do as they pleased. Prostitutes went to the falls to work, soldiers and "factory girls" went to meet and carouse and drink. Young men from the city, jealous of the attention the soldiers got from the young ladies, went to the pavilions to pick fights.

On the other hand, the neighborhood people, on their large lots and in their big houses, wanted the quiet enjoyment of their homes. The streetcar crowds were far too festive and free for those proper ladies. One even considered sending a formal complaint demanding more security to Thomas Lowry and his streetcar company. The *Minneapolis Tribune* complained—as ever—that rowdyism by this undisciplined crowd was ruining the park.

Just eight days after the newspaper story, in the moonless night of August 14, the Cass and Gardner pavilion and dance hall caught fire and burned to the ground.

The fire started in the hall, not at the other end of the building where nine people slept. All escaped with the clothes on their backs and little else, but the place was a total wreck. The pavilion had been closed for a few days because Sophia Cass had suddenly died, aged thirty-three, of unknown causes. Louis and their three children had just returned from the trip to Iowa where they buried her. According to both the *St. Paul Globe* and the *Minneapolis Tribune*, the fire was surely set. The *Globe* headline brought home the point about arson: "Neighbors Hated It." Louis Cass lost everything he owned in the fire, and he had no insurance. The three Cass children were made motherless and homeless in the same week.[16]

The Gardners carry on with the carryings-on

Twelve days later, Irwin Gardner took out a building permit for a new thirty-by-eighty-foot pavilion. Like the Cass pavilion, this was on Vinette Lincoln's land. Most of her property adjacent to the park had been sitting empty for all these years. Closest to the falls and just opposite the Milwaukee depot were lots 3–11, Runyan's Addition. These nine lots became the heart of the Minnehaha Midway: a row of pavilions, games, rides, and dance halls that faced the park.

Vinette gave a lease on all of it to Adelbert's adult son, Irwin A. Gardner. Adelbert was married to Emma Bacon, and both of them were from Brookfield, New York. Their only child, Irwin, was twenty-three years old in 1895; Irwin and his wife, Clara, had a baby son named Louis. The Gardner pavilion was a substantial structure with rooms upstairs where all five family members lived.

Once the Gardners built their new pavilion in late 1895, they settled into running their "resort" at the falls. Foster, Babcock, Poudler, and a few others were all in business. Things were quiet enough. Minnehaha Park was constantly used for church or union picnics, and for dances at the park board picnic pavilion. The Gardners were still in business with Louis Cass, and they quietly continued to operate. There was no hint of scandal from Babcock's operation, either.

That's not to say they were entirely aboveboard. In 1897, a police roundup at the pavilions resulted in the arrest of Irwin Gardner, Sidney Babcock, Robert E. Fischer, and a couple of other confectioners, including Abbie Burlingame, a clerk working for the Foster pavilion. Almost everyone except Poudler got busted for selling alcohol without a license. Burlingame sat in jail waiting for Andrew Foster—an

In about 1895, behind the three behatted women sitting among the flowers, two pavilions can be seen past the south portico of the Milwaukee depot. To the left is the well-signed Cass confectionary; beyond the pillars of the portico, a man stands in front of the dancing pavilion run by the Gardners. *MNHS*

otherwise well-respected citizen—to pay her seventy-five-dollar fine. Fischer, who had been a policeman with both the city and the park police, certainly knew better. He and Irwin Gardner both paid the seventy-five-dollar fines themselves. Babcock tried to get out of it by presenting a document from a brewery certifying that the "fizz" he sold was non-intoxicating, but the court was having none of it. He was fined twenty-five dollars or thirty days. The judge, apparently convinced that Babcock was a slightly more upstanding citizen (like John Booth in the previous generation), fined him less than the others. Perhaps after the Cass and Gardner pavilion burned to the ground, Babcock toned things down.[17]

Things drifted along for a few more years as Vinette Lincoln's strip of land outside Minnehaha Park got more crowded with pavilions.

Wild behavior began to ratchet up. At some point, Gardner's pavilion was increased in size from 80 to 150 feet long. The Gardners catered to the obvious desire people had to gather, mingle, dance, and drink.

Sidney Babcock died in January 1899, and his wife quickly remarried and moved to Saskatchewan. Even without Babcock, the season of 1899 at Minnehaha was a notoriously rowdy one. The Gardners' dance hall became the scene of even more debauchery. By the end of June 1899, they were back in court. Irwin and Adelbert Gardner and a man named "C. Lewis" (probably Louis Cass) found themselves sued by the city for running a disorderly house, their pavilion at the falls.

Once again, the neighborhood grew weary of disruptive dances and licentious, dissipated behavior. The neighbors in their fine homes near the falls convinced the city attorney to bring charges. Record-breaking crowds showed up in Judge Andrew Holt's tiny, dingy courtroom to testify for and against the goings-on at Gardner's pavilion at Minnehaha. The *Tribune* ran a detailed account of the proceedings on June 28, 1899: "The entire Minnehaha Improvement Association turned out, the park police also, streetcar conductors, old soldiers from the home: all classes were represented, even the girls who participated in the social parties were present to uphold the reputation of Gardner's place. There were numbers of fair beings who have sometimes lost themselves in the mazes of the dance, who were there to tell what a nice place Gardner's resort was. There were men of the Bowery variety there also, to add their good words to the others in behalf of the place of recreation."

People living near the falls have been "obliged to submit to insults at the hands of habitués, have had their ears assailed with the noise of scrap and wassail, have been obliged to be referees in fights on streetcars, and have dodged blows nightly on their trips in and out of town. They say they have borne more than they will bear again." The details came out. Women as young as fourteen or fifteen were dancing a little too close to men they did not know. Prostitutes offered more than that: "The bargain and sale of personal charms [were] heard on the still night air." Liquor was not openly offered for sale; the leases from Vinette Lincoln prohibited it. But men carried their bottles and flasks regardless. There was plenty of booze around.

During the trial, witnesses from the neighborhood overwhelmed the court with complaints and stories about the intemperate behavior

In June 28, 1899, the Minneapolis Tribune *ran this cartoon by R. C. Bowman with a parody of Longfellow's* Song of Hiawatha *by Oscar F. G. Day, in which Minnehaha returns to the falls.*

> She returned, but sad to tell it, gone was
>   all the old-time splendor,
> Greeted her ears with noises, while
>   some neophyte musicians
> Scraped upon the quivering catgut, till
>   the very air was shivered;
> And the shocking hobo laughter caused
>   the very trees to shudder.
>
> All around was wild carousal—beer was
>   foaming, men were swearing—
> Maidens in their teens were dancing with
>   the veriest abandon—
> Lingerie was elevated, shrieks were there of
>   drunken orgie—
> Men were pasted, others battered, and the
>   free fights that she saw there
> Broke the heart of Minnehaha.

THE SPIRIT OF MINNEHAHA.

at Gardner's pavilion and on the streetcars. James R. Hartzell, who ran a grocery store next to Foster's pavilion at East 50th Street and 43rd Avenue South, testified against the Gardners. On the night of June 20, there was so much disruptive noise from the dance hall that he walked over to see what was going on. "'There was hollering and some shooting. I walked down to the hall and looked in, and I heard foul language and swearing.' Assistant City Attorney H. Danforth Dickinson asked, 'What did they say?' to which Hartzell replied that he 'would not like to say. Men were there who carried liquor with them, and they drank it on the premises. And I have seen gambling there on Mr. Gardner's grounds.'"

All the witnesses refused to repeat the highly offensive language overheard, but many claimed that the women swore worse than the men. Many testified that the dancing was too intimate. The neighbors were so deeply offended that even people who should have been the Gardners' allies testified against them. William R. Dobbyn took the stand. His was a respected voice in the Populist Party, and he surely knew Adelbert Gardner from that work. Yet he told the court, "I could not believe that human beings could act so. It was beyond belief, and I hate to tell you, for fear you will scarcely believe the story I tell, it is so incredible." Mr. Frank R. Hubacheck (for the defense): "Were the men drunk?" "I think they were." "What makes you think so?" "Because they were full of whisky." "How do you know they were full of whisky?" shouted Hubacheck. "Because I saw them pour it into themselves." When Dobbyn's son Deronda was on the stand, he testified that during the dance men and women were embracing in an indiscriminate fashion. Mr. Hubacheck: "Well they put their arms about women at society dances, don't they?" "Yes, but they don't hug them so tight." "Were they being handled in any unseemly way?" "I should say they were."

The prosecution simply deluged the other side with evidence. They called many others who lived in the neighborhood, all respected citizens. One was district court judge Alexander M. Harrison; another was state senator Sylvanus A. Stockwell. Stockwell was a social liberal and another who ought to have allied with Adelbert Gardner's politics, but he wanted nothing to do with this noisy, rowdy hot spot and its indiscriminate proprietors. That Stockwell had been raised in the temperance movement surely influenced his decision to testify against Gardner; Harrison's wife was also prominent in the Women's Christian Temperance Union.

The prosecution also called prostitutes to the stand: "Some of the female denizens of the tenderloin district told what went on at the pavilion and on [the streetcars], and it was about as shocking a recital as one could hear in a civilized community." Clearly having the sex workers testify did the Gardners no favors. The *Tribune* commented, "Amidst all this were young people of both sexes, scarcely more than children, who were becoming apprenticed in the life led by older women who frequent the place." In his summation, Judge Andrew Holt said, "There is evidence here that many men of the best class attend this pavilion and participate in the dances, but it is noticeable that the wives of those men are conspicuous by their absence. Those kinds of places are necessarily visited by people of loose character, and they do not know how to behave in a proper manner. . . . Men go there for the purpose of assisting in the ruin of young girls." It was an additional affront that all this was going on at Minnehaha Falls, a place that still had great, emotional, romantic resonance with the public.

It wasn't just the noise, gambling, public drunkenness, lewd dancing, and prostitution that so offended those living near the park. What really upset the neighbors was how completely uninhabitable the streetcars had become on the line to and from Minnehaha. The streetcars leaving Minnehaha in the evening—especially those leaving the pavilion after midnight when the dance had ended—were filled with disgraceful "toughs" engaged in bad language, drinking, and vice. Women, some quite young, rode the car back to the city, and some drank from whiskey bottles that the men passed around. Many people, even women, smoked cigarettes. People sang, and they talked loudly, making filthy lewd remarks. The conductor could do nothing about this.

Often the behavior was worse: they smashed windows, scratched seats, and pulled the register cord—the device the conductor used to record fares as he collected them. When a large crowd boarded, the toughs would not pay their fares, and then they threatened to throw the conductor overboard. Clearly, it was unsafe for respectable women to ride the streetcars at late hours. And this was the main transportation everyone in the falls neighborhood used to go back and forth to the city. The neighbors relied on the streetcars, filled with rowdy drunken debauchery or not.

The judge's verdict reflected the public sentiment that none of this behavior was acceptable. Judge Holt ruled that Adelbert Gardner did not own the dance hall and therefore was not responsible for what happened there. Perhaps this was nothing more than a transactional decision: the family would pay one fine instead of two. (Whatever the nature of the father-son relationship between the Gardners—and it is not well documented—Adelbert was indeed the boss of the dance hall.) The judge fined "C. Lewis" (Louis Cass) and Irwin Gardner each eighty days in jail or seventy-five dollars. Police Superintendent James G. Doyle declared himself ready to show up with the paddy wagon if any unseemly behavior broke out at the Gardners' pavilion. That ought to have been the end of that.[18]

7

Corruption Reigns

I NIQUITY WAS NOT THE GARDNERS' ONLY VOCATION. In addition to running the dance hall, Adelbert had stayed at least peripherally connected to politics and populism. In 1897, for example, he turned up at organizing meetings for the Populist Party. There, he might have met Doc Ames, who was also in the thick of the Populist effort at the time. If the two men hadn't already known one another from GAR functions or from crossing paths in one of Minnehaha's wild dance halls, they absolutely would have become acquainted in one of the Merchants Hotel's smoky rooms, where the party gathered to strategize over the upcoming 1898 elections.

That year, the Populists joined forces with the Democrats to put "Honest John" Lind in the governor's mansion. Ames also made another run for Minneapolis mayor—this time as an independent—and Adelbert surely helped on the campaign. The working people of Minneapolis had always been Ames's strongest supporters, and Adelbert had spent his entire career as a political organizer trying to empower that same group of people. Though the doctor eventually lost to the Democrat James Gray, the 1898 campaign surely cemented the relationship Ames had with both the Gardners.

Two years later, Ames ran for mayor again, this time taking advantage of the new Minnesota direct primary law, which had passed in 1899. The law was designed to reform elections, and it allowed voters (instead of convention delegates) to choose their own candidates for the general election. Though the law restricted voters to a single party, it was left up to them to declare their own party affiliation and request the appropriate ballot. In this campaign cycle, Ames decided to run as a Republican against Gray, who had outpolled him nearly four to one in their 1898 contest. Gray was popular, but Ames thought he might be able to combine his own working-class supporters with the solid, business-oriented Republican voters and defeat him. He was right, and on January 7, 1901, Doc Ames was sworn in for the fourth time as mayor of Minneapolis.[1]

During the open primary, Ames had carried 75 percent of the vote in the Twelfth Ward, the neighborhoods that surround Minnehaha Falls. Undoubtedly, the Gardners had provided invaluable help in that area, politicking to recruit voters and secure Ames's place on the ballot. The residents of the Soldiers' Home knew Ames not just as a fellow veteran but as their doctor, so they supported him as well.

After his victory, Ames was ready to give back to the supporters who had helped put him in office. He particularly intended to thank a number of shady characters who could help turn his final administration into a graft operation designed to line his pockets. There had been hints of criminal behavior in Ames's previous administrations, but after the election of 1900, he lost all restraint. He hired gamblers and criminals in top positions and focused on making as much money for himself as possible. He also went to work dismantling and debasing the city's police department—replacing most of the force with biddable, corrupt men; this included the return of Charlie Hill as first precinct commander—so the force would either ignore or participate in his criminal schemes.[2]

Adelbert and Irwin Gardner were both given positions in Ames's new city government. Adelbert became Minneapolis's saloon license inspector, and his job was to make sure the establishments that were offering alcohol for sale were doing so legally. Irwin was, perhaps improbably, a medical student, and was working with Ames in the doctor's medical and surgical practice, and had been for a few years. He became the mayor's special assistant. This new position wasn't related to medicine, however, but to politics.

As part of his new job, Irwin collected "fees" from the city's prostitutes. Minneapolis had de facto licensed sex work since the 1870s, with fees paid monthly in court. As mayor, though, Ames made it clear that those monthly court appearances would no longer be necessary. Instead, the "public women" would pay a fee in court every other month, and in between those appearances, Irwin would go around and collect another set of fees, which he then turned over

Irwin Gardner, 1901, from a photo of the Minneapolis police amateur baseball team. Irwin was the team's manager. *HCL*

to the mayor. Irwin wasn't an official member of the police force, but Ames gave him a policeman's star to wear while performing his assigned duties. This corruption cut one of the city's revenue sources in half, even as it sent thousands of dollars directly to Mayor Ames.[3]

The Gardners continued operating their pavilion, though the entire family moved to 512 Tenth Avenue South (where the U.S. Bank Stadium sits today). Considering Irwin's familiarity with public women, the family's former rooms at the pavilion might have been the scene of paid-for sex. He also continued to hold the lease on lots 3–11 of Vinette Lincoln's land in Runyan's Addition. With the certainty that city hall would not interfere, it's no wonder that the number of pavilions in the area began to grow. Irwin controlled access to the Lincoln land, collected rents, and let the mayhem continue.

The new strip, including other establishments not on Vinette's lots 3–11 and not under Irwin's control, came to be known as the Minnehaha Midway. These places were objectionable in part because they were temporary, seasonal shacks that looked garish and grubby. Many businesses seemed innocent enough. They sold peanuts, ice cream, or lunch to visitors at the falls. One of the veterans living at the Soldiers' Home ran a tintype photograph operation. There were souvenir stands, shooting galleries, and "fakir's booths" (which probably ran sideshow games or small performances). Nearly all of these establishments were seasonal, and many of them didn't last for more than a few years. Naturally, many of the people who operated the pavilions sold alcohol illegally, and they were regularly fined for it. And even after the arsonist's fire had destroyed Cass's pavilion, little changed with the new Gardner pavilion in terms of the shenanigans that transpired there.

MERRILY GOING AROUND—OR NOT

The midway became more carnival-like than ever when a Ferris wheel and a merry-go-round were brought in.

The merry-go-round was an especial attraction. These rides were rather new to the public in Minnesota in the 1890s. Small-town newspapers reported that thousands of people turned up to see this new device and to ride the horses.

The merry-go-round arrived on the Minnehaha Midway in 1903. There are no reports of gleeful children at Minnehaha: quite the contrary. The merry-go-round had, as should be expected, several different proprietors and owners. It ran from an engine that belched black smoke, and it "destroyed the Sunday quiet for blocks," which deeply angered a man named James Galehouse, who lived about four blocks away. Galehouse joined with other neighbors to suppress the nuisance of the merry-go-round. They used the same strategy the residents of Richfield had previously employed to stifle liquor sales. Proactively, these neighborhood people went to the scene of the objectional behavior, gathered evidence, and took it to the police. The merry-go-round's engineer was fined for "violating the smoke ordinance." Owner Chas Bazine said he had a city-issued permit for the merry-go-round. He did move the ride across the street, but had no intention of shutting it down. He seems to have sold it to Edward Parks, who owned a saloon downtown.[4]

The smoke and noise were not the real issue, at least not for Miss Alice Johnson. A couple of weeks after the nuisance complaint, the police picked up the merry-go-round's ticket taker and its owner, Edward Parks, on "a serious charge" that had been made by this fifteen-year-old girl and her mother.[5]

Alice had been out late at night for several weeks, and on Thursday she visited the falls and did not return home. Police help was called for; the detective learned that she remained near the park all night and had been riding the merry-go-round on Friday morning. Bail was set at $1,500 each for the ticket taker and Parks, who, in addition

The Minneapolis Tribune *of August 17, 1894, was effusively enthusiastic about the delights of merry-go-rounds.*

No other sight is more inspiring of gentle feelings than that of a lot of little girls and little boys seated in the coaches and upon the horses of a revolving merry-go-round. What noble horses they are! Was there ever a more extraordinary combination of attractive colors? Can you estimate the joy of a child that is permitted to mount and ride a magnificent wooden equine, painted a brilliant red, with jet black ears, fiery blue eyes, a tail and mane of real green hair and with a saddle and bridle of honest engine leather, beautifully embellished with gold and silver? The most remarkable feature of it all is that each horse is better than the others—if you doubt it, just ask the little folk themselves. . . . The music, too, adds to the excitement and the charm. It seems to come from an inner circle, a kind of holy of holies that is screened off in such wise that we have never been able to discover how the music is actually made, although we have distinct suspicions on that point. It inspires not only the little women and the little men, but also the red horses and the blue horses and the other horses and sometimes—yes, actually sometimes, while that merry-go-round went twirling and humming like a big grand top, while the music behind the curtain went "ump-yah, ump-yah, ump-yah," oh, ever so sweetly, and while the boys and girls shouted and laughed and made other gleeful demonstrations, why then—this is true what we tell you, we have heard those horses neigh and whinny with delight.

The passions of youth do not altogether die with the years. There are merry-go-rounds to amuse every age and every condition; everybody rides, and hidden music goes "ump-yah" "ump-yah." This is a beautiful world and human life is well worth living.

to his saloon, ran a pavilion near the falls and that merry-go-round. He had hired the girl to work in his pavilion, and she had told him she was only fifteen. The grand jury eventually examined the charge "criminal knowledge of a child" and let them go for unexplained reasons, possibly owing to mutual hatred between the grand jury members and the county attorney. Separately, Parks lost his liquor license for his downtown saloon, as he had to explain to the authorities, first, why he invited the fifteen-year-old girl into his saloon and, second, what was going on at the pavilion he kept at Minnehaha Falls.

Ownership of the merry-go-round fell next to Charles C. Patten, and there are no wild stories about his operation. He had been a park policeman in Minnehaha Park, during which time the paper reported that he "had a truck farm, a candy store and a boarding stable, ran a bus line to Fort Snelling and back, ran two ice wagons, and bought a little real estate. He dabbled in the amusement business, too, while he was on the force." Patten seems to have been a pretty nice guy, but one wonders about all the extracurricular goings-on with the park police. He went on to have a carnival that he toured through the west and even into Canada. He was known as "the Sunday School Carnival Man," an allusion to the basically honest show he toured: no shifty hustlers with his carnival.[6]

With his brother serving as police chief, Doc Ames corrupted the city government and enriched himself. But the operation soon got out of control, and the fourth and final Ames administration didn't last long. Six months into 1901, the public was increasingly concerned about their city. A grand jury convened to examine how known criminals were arrested and just turned loose again, how new gambling establishments were being set up under police protection, why quasi-legal prostitution was happening, and similar matters. Ames's corruption included installing unqualified but loyal people in positions of power. The newspapers pointed out that Adelbert Gardner was in no way qualified for his job checking saloon licenses. Gardner allowed licenses to be transferred from one saloon to another, and in this way men secured licenses who could not otherwise qualify for them.[7]

Gardner claimed he was being persecuted because of his friendship with Ames, but he resigned in August of 1902. Ames followed him a few weeks after that. Irwin was indicted—the charge was collecting bribes from prostitutes—and sentenced to six years in prison. Although the fourth and final Ames administration didn't last long, the trials went on for years.[8]

Wild behavior was under scrutiny in the courts, and it's easy to imagine that the Gardners' rowdy, anything-goes dance hall and the other pavilions outside the park would have no future in this reform era. But out at Minnehaha, the Gardners' political influence was still strong, and in 1902, the midway endured. In the city directory from

The Ferris wheel at Minnehaha, about 1902. *Photo by Joe Riggs, HHM*

that year, ten "confectioners" are listed, all located on the small strip of land opposite the park. The Lincolns must have been making a fortune, and Vinette must have noticed that her lessees, the Gardners, were looking like an increasingly disreputable bunch. She surely needed the income from renting her land, but she also had a social position to think about. There was an obvious solution to this quandary. As the grand jury started handing out sheaves of indictments,

Vinette's youngest daughter, Fanny Grace, escorted her mother to Maine to visit relatives. Vinette would remain back East for four years. Her older daughters were gone from the scene at Minnehaha. Bertha had left the country to teach in the Philippines a few months previously, and Florence had married for the second time, would soon be widowed again, and no longer had a share in the land.[9]

ATTACKING THE MIDWAY

The war over control of the park would heat up. Literally. On October 29, 1904, flames again lit the night sky, and competition between a vendor in the park and those on its borders was the likely motivation for this fire. The target? The park board had built a pavilion of its own.

The park board's commissioners began to think about building a public pavilion in 1902 as a way to take business away from the Minnehaha Midway shacks. It was a seasonal refreshment pavilion like the ones outside the park. The park board called its building the refectory. The name would differentiate the new building from those other pavilions, with their increasingly unseemly connotations. By the end of that year, a man named Harry Barnet convinced the board to allow him to build and operate a new facility at Minnehaha Falls for the 1903 season.[10]

Harry and Jacob Barnet were brothers who ran concessions at various parks around the Twin Cities. Harry was known and trusted by the park board; he had been running an electric merry-go-round at Lake Harriet since at least 1893. He also managed a dance pavilion at Wildwood Amusement Park on White Bear Lake. Jacob, his younger brother, stayed in the park concessions business longer, especially at Como Park in St. Paul. It was Jacob who ultimately built and ran the refreshment pavilion in Minnehaha Park. The story is a bit murky, but it seems that in the winter of 1902, Harry was given the privilege— and then the commissioners changed their minds.

The park board is often not the most straightforward or transparent of operations. In 1903, as soon as the newly elected commissioners were sworn in, they reconsidered the matter. During months of contentious dithering, the board rejected entire rounds of bids, decided to set prices for the refreshments on offer at the park, and generally vacillated.

When they put the project out for bids a second time, they attracted a bid from John Dreher, who managed a pavilion on the midway. Unsurprisingly, he did not win, losing out to Jacob Barnet. Deeply upset, Dreher took the floor at a park board meeting and loudly insisted that he be awarded the bid. His bid was lower than Barnet's; by the rules of the request for proposals, he felt he was entitled to the contract, and he demanded it. He brought to the meeting a cadre of supporters to make some noise on his behalf, but the board was not swayed. Some commissioners who had sided with Barnet—the final tally was six to four—said they had voted for the more experienced man. But if the vote was a symbolic repudiation of the rowdies operating outside the park, those rowdies would have more to say to the park board in the coming years.

Barnet paid for the construction of the new building. It was a rectangular hall with covered porches, a simple and pretty design by architect and park board member Harry Wild Jones. Barnet opened the refectory in the spring of 1903. The building was sited on the picturesque point overlooking the falls from the east. That's where the Song of Hiawatha garden is located today and where Harriet Eves (Collar) had had her restaurant in the 1880s.

From the beginning, there were concerns that the refectory was too small. Including the piazza outside, it was only forty feet by sixty

The first refectory, built by Harry Barnet, about 1903. *Photo by Elgin Shepard, HHM*

feet. When it opened on May 24, the *Tribune* reported that the crowds were the "largest ever" and "completely overwhelmed the place." Every streetcar was "loaded to the guards," and by 9 AM, every seat at every table was taken.[11]

Barnet put up awnings to provide more shaded seating. He also advertised for the dozens of employees he needed to help run the place. In a single week, he needed twenty waiters, a cook, two dining girls, two cashiers, two dishwashers, and a slew of salesladies and pantry girls.[12]

The new refectory was so popular that the park board thought it might ask the streetcar company to extend its tracks another half mile south along Minnehaha Avenue, making it easier for crowds to use the southern part of the park. All in all, the refectory looked to be a splendid success. Not everyone loved it, however.

FIGHTING BACK AGAINST THE MIDWAY PAVILIONS, STEP I

The park board's refectory did a good job in competing with the well-established party scene on the midway. Still, neighborhood men of wealth and influence encouraged the park board to get directly involved in stamping out the midway rowdies. Since the pavilions were on the park's western edge and clearly not within the park proper, the board had no jurisdiction over them. But it jumped into the fracas anyway.

The park board took an important step in controlling the rowdyism on the edge of the park when it acquired a different strip of land, owned by the heirs of Franklin Steele. The Godfrey Tract, a two-hundred-foot strip just north of the park, is populated today by horseshoe pits and picnic grounds. It is separated from the rest of the park by the Godfrey Parkway and has never seemed to be fully a part of Minnehaha Park.[13]

The procedure to condemn the strip proceeded relatively quickly in 1903. Acquiring the Godfrey Tract was an expense, but it did not involve a battle. Franklin Steele's seven remaining adult children owned the land, and after accepting their payments, they handed over the title without much fuss. Katherine, one of Steele's daughters, asked for her family's home—that home that had been lived in by the Steeles, the Lincolns, Captain John Tapper, and unidentified parties running a shady business, but the park board refused. (Eventually it was sold to Charles Patten, the Sunday School Carnival Man, who moved it to 5028 Hiawatha and lived in it for many years. He kept his trained bear, trained goat, and other animals in an outbuilding on his property when they were not on the road. The house still stands.)[14]

Some "shacks and stands" along the Godfrey Strip were shut down, including the sweet pea–growing business of Harriet Eves (Collar). After this strategic acquisition on the northern edge of the park, when the final assault was made on the midway on the west side of the park, those businesses would have no place to go.[15]

THERE'S A LAW AGAINST THAT

The refectory's popularity did not go unnoticed by Adelbert Gardner and the other pavilion keepers on the midway. It was clear that the park board's attempt to take away their business was a success. They announced their intentions to retaliate by bringing legal action against the park board and Jacob Barnet. The accusation was that Barnet (and, by extension, the board) were illegally selling items on Sunday, and that those sales were of prohibited items.[16]

The blue laws that had tripped up proprietors at the falls in the 1870s were back in play. In 1903, the list of items whose sale on Sunday was prohibited included "uncooked meats, fish, salt, groceries, dry goods, clothing, apparel of any kind, boots, or shoes." (The Retail Clerks' Association had much to do with this list.) Likewise, the law actually specified those items that could legally be sold on Sunday: "meals may be sold to be eaten upon the premises where sold, or served elsewhere by caterers, and prepared tobacco in places other than where wine or spirituous liquors are sold, and fruits, drugs, confectionary, newspapers, medicines and surgical supplies may be sold in a quiet and orderly manner."

The Gardners and the other pavilion keepers outside the park noticed that the law didn't allow for the sale of pop, cookies, ice cream, and lemonade, all of which Barnet had on offer at the refectory. "If the lines become tensely drawn," opined the newspaper, "there will be arrests if any of those are sold on Sunday." Nothing much seems to have come of this threat. Ultimately, the park board wasn't interested in shutting down a moneymaking operation. The board was proud of its own pavilion, saying it was "a gem of its kind, and it provides a place where refreshments of a clean and wholesome nature may be procured at a reasonable cost."[17]

Still, the refectory and Jacob Barnet had to deal with detractors. In 1903, an unknown someone invited the Minnesota dairy commissioners (who had also become food safety inspectors) to look into some—but not all—of the pavilions at Minnehaha. The most likely culprits to have made that call were the Gardners. During a tenure as a lecturer for the Farmers' Alliance in the 1880s, Adelbert Gardner was also a cheesemaker at a large creamery; he would have been aware of the dairy commissioners. Attention was focused on Barnet's operation as well as William Poudler's, and the inspectors found that all the ciders they sold were adulterated. Barnet made his own soda fountain syrups and Poudler bought his; many of those also did not pass inspection.[18]

Barnet was also brought to court for selling alcohol without a license. His defense was that he was using a claret flavoring syrup that contained the intoxicant, but that he was not actually serving alcohol. Judge Holt, who had presided over Irwin Gardner's disorderly house conviction in 1899, was familiar with the illegal goings-on at the park. Impatient over the recurrence of such shenanigans, he fined Barnet fifty dollars. Adelbert Gardner, having been fired from his position as Doc Ames's (saloon) license inspector, might well have had an opinion on legal and illegal alcohol sales, and he just might have brought it to the park police force's attention.[19]

The park board also scrutinized Barnet's "clean and wholesome refreshments" in 1904, when a number of commissioners (Charles Loring, John H. van Nest, Fred L. Smith, and Jesse E. Northrup) decided to examine the refectory's water supply. During construction of the refectory, the board had drilled a well and built a spring water tank to provide for Barnet's shop. Iron pipes and a gasoline engine pump carried water from the well to the tank. A separate plumbing setup used creek water to sprinkle the flower beds in the park. These commissioners, with odd and single-minded acuity, examined this setup and discovered a simple valve that allowed water to be drawn directly from the creek into the refectory drinking water supply. Barnet claimed he didn't know anything about this. In fact, he probably didn't—he seems not to have been mechanically minded. (Barnet began his career at Minnehaha advertising for a gasoline engine, then he advertised for a man who knew how to run a gasoline engine. Eventually, after the fire, he advertised salvage on the gasoline engine.)[20]

This was just another way that Barnet's business was assailed by unseen antagonists who wished him ill. In this case, it was likely the park policeman, John F. O'Brien, who had alerted the park board. His story is told below.

THE USUAL SOLUTION TO PROBLEMS AT MINNEHAHA

In the spring of 1904, Barnet submitted a plan for a waiting room near the streetcar stop on the south side of the creek. He was asking to build a rather large building, 3,400 square feet, with seats for those who were waiting for the streetcar and room enough for him to serve "light refreshments"—peanuts and cool drinks and such. Surely, the refectory's overwhelming popularity made it obvious that more money could be made at Minnehaha. All signs pointed to the next season being more profitable than the last, and the park board could have welcomed this opportunity to increase its income. Instead, Barnet's plan went to a committee for consideration.[21]

Seated from right, Jacob Barnet, unidentified child, superintendent William M. Berry, and commissioner Jesse E. Northrup, about 1903. The others, all park board members, are not identified. *Western Camera Publishing Company, MNHS*

Barnet forged ahead and built his stand without the park board's authorization. We have no map or record of its location, but it seems to have been south of the creek, placed there to attract crowds as they exited the streetcar or train and walked toward the falls. (If Minnehaha Park ever had a main entrance, this would have been it.) Some of the board's members felt they couldn't allow Barnet to get away with building his own peanut stand. William Berry, the board's superintendent, commented that it "would be a gathering place of big crowds with the result that the lawn would be trampled down and the spot littered with paper bags, boxes, and other debris." The board had put considerable expense into beautifying this part of the park, and Charles Loring, another board member, was especially unhappy. His objection was that this most cherished park was not the appropriate place for Mr. Barnet's business ventures. The rest of the board seemingly saw the value in Barnet's ideas, however, and voted against Loring and Berry's wishes, though they fined Barnet two hundred dollars for building without permission.[22]

The 1904 season played out with Barnet doing his best to supply the demand for refreshments in the park. He continued to advertise for dozens of workers. By October, his refectory was only open on Sundays, squeezing out the last few days for those who wanted to enjoy Minnesota's glorious autumn weather.

On October 27, 1904, the last Friday of the month, the park board's refectory burned to the ground. Since no one lived particularly close by, the fire grew large before anyone noticed it. By the time neighbors arrived, the flames were spreading quickly. Bystanders tried to salvage what they could of the tables and chairs and other items inside. Someone said kerosene had been sprinkled around. Someone telephoned the fire department, but there was no fire station in this farthest southeast corner of Minneapolis, so the response took a while. And when the firefighters finally arrived, they discovered they had no way to get water to their hoses.[23]

The fire had started around 10 PM. Long before morning, the park board's refectory was a smoldering heap of ashes and charred timber. In the war over control of the park, arson was once again used to someone's advantage. The refectory's run ended after two short seasons. No injuries were reported—except, perhaps, to the prospects of Jacob Barnet. At least in this case, the park board had insurance.

And who lit the fire? John Dreher might have held a grudge all this time. But Adelbert Gardner, running the Minnehaha Midway, was the prime suspect. It was Gardner who had both a pavilion and a leasing arrangement with several other shady operators, Gardner who promoted unsavory dances, and Gardner who allowed and profited from the mayhem. Nothing was ever proven against him.

REBUILDING: A NEW REFECTORY

A few weeks after the refectory went up in flames, the park board began planning to replace it. The board called for architects to submit designs, and from twelve choices, they picked a building of cement and stucco. It was guaranteed to be fireproof.

The design came from the firm of Downs and Eads, not (for once) Harry Wild Jones. It was described as "Spanish style" due to its red tile roof, "graceful, substantial and convenient. Nature's green relieved by a touch of red." The board decided to build the refectory on the high open ground just north of the bridge above the falls, much closer to the corner of Godfrey Road and Minnehaha Avenue, and near the 1892 picnic pavilion. It is still standing today.[24]

Running a refreshment concession in the Minneapolis parks is a seasonal business, and once spring is here in earnest, there is not a moment to be lost. Construction began in April of 1905 and the refectory was ready for business by July. Though the board needed someone to run the place, and asked for bids from potential concessionaires,

The second refectory, which still stands, about 1905

Barnet didn't apply. Perhaps he had had enough of inspectors, accusations, fines, and fires.

The winning bid was submitted by a man named Harry H. Green. He was the son of an immigrant junk peddler who had become a pawnbroker and then a jeweler; he ran his own jewelry store on Seventh between Hennepin and Nicollet into the 1950s and until he was nearly ninety years old. He was just as interested in "show business" as he was in the jewelry trade. He built Minneapolis's first movie theater and ran it for decades. He also produced various plays and shows that were immensely successful. He brought some of that same theatrical flair to Minnehaha Falls when he applied for permission to illuminate the falls at night, just as Captain Palmer had done forty years earlier. Harry Green lit the waterfall from behind—it was incorrectly reported that it was the first time that had ever been done—and it drew huge crowds all throughout July.[25]

His penchant for the dramatic was a great help, but Green didn't come to the refectory with experience in food service. Conveniently, though, he had a source for that kind of expertise; his sister Annie was married to Jacob Barnet. Green was in business as quickly as possible. Even before construction on the new refectory was completed, he was already serving refreshments at Barnet's old waiting-room peanut stand.

FIGHTING BACK AGAINST THE MIDWAY PAVILIONS, STEP 2

Let us be clear—many of the people living in the surrounding neighborhoods hated the Minnehaha Midway. This was a class issue, a racist issue (as various complaints would show), an issue of moral buttoned-up certitude taking the high ground to stare at dissipated carefreeness with condemning eyes and horrified attitude. Those who moved to the new districts near the falls knew what the scene was; they just intended to put a stop to it.

During the years when the pavilion keepers were fighting with the park board, from 1903 through 1905, a series of even more startling actions and reactions were taking place with the neighborhood and the city. The refectory took some business from the midway, but the midway continued to prosper. The community's most prominent men enlisted the Commercial Club in their cause. They had already petitioned the park board to acquire the remaining strip of Runyan's Addition, and with the Godfrey Tract in hand and the trials of Ames and his accomplices in full swing, the time was right for a little reformation at Minnehaha.[26]

The Gardners and the businesses that subleased from them, in hopes of staving off the inevitable, tried toning down their most raucous behavior. But the neighbors had had enough. And even though city hall was figuratively a smoldering ruin after the Ames trials, and even though the park board didn't have jurisdiction over nonpark lands, the wealthier people in the surrounding neighborhoods had another card to play in their quest to rid the park of the pavilions. The Commercial Club asked the Milwaukee Road to put up a six-foot-tall fence to the west of its right-of-way, making it impossible for crowds to reach the midway from the tracks.[27]

When the pavilion owners, led by Irwin Gardner, found out about the plans, they went to court to get an injunction to stop the fence's construction. After spending the last year on the witness stand testifying against Ames and his former machine, and after being convicted himself of six counts of receiving bribes, you might think that by this time, Irwin would have been tired of courtrooms and judges.

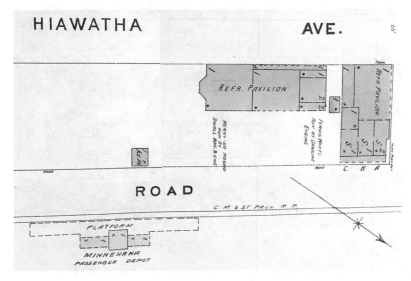

The Rascher insurance map shows the locations of the merry-go-round, the Ferris wheel, and the Milwaukee depot, about 1903. Gardner's "highway by prescription" is the space between the two large pavilions. *MNHS*

He initially argued that the new fence was on his property. When that argument didn't pan out, he then claimed that an easement existed. The fence was illegally blocking a pathway across the property, which Gardner called a "highway by prescription." Though the pavil-

On July 9, 1903, the *Minneapolis Journal* ran these three images under the headline, "The Pavilion Situation at Minnehaha." A caption noted that "A stout wire fence has been erected along the edge of the Milwaukee road's right of way, leaving only a few feet in front of the pavilions in the space where crowds of patrons have been

ion owners offered many affidavits from neighbors swearing that the pathway across the midway had existed for decades, on June 30, 1903, the fence went up, west of the tracks that ran behind the Milwaukee depot.[28]

wont to congregate. The resorts are still accessible, but they cannot continue in business with only a narrow alley in front." The top photo shows the area before the fence was erected. At lower left, workers unroll the fencing; at lower right, the result. *Photos by Arus S. Williams*

This fence blocked access to all the confectioneries except for William Poudler's Blue Star Pavilion, which was located at the north end of the group, just at 49th Street. The fence did not continue past his property, and his pavilion was the first that customers could reach after crossing the tracks. With his newfound popularity, it took him only a week to expand his business so that it covered the whole corner. Even with the fence in place, the neighborhood still complained about noise on Sunday, and the newspapers reported that "On Sundays it is 'alive with refreshment vendors, colored singers and gramophones.'"[29]

For what seemed like the hundredth time in the long battle to control the sale of alcohol, the community residents agitated to get the Sunday selling law enforced. As the citizens of Richfield had done twenty years before, they organized searches of the pavilions to look for evidence of illegal activity, and they planned to swear out warrants with the city attorney.

The other pavilion keepers saw their livelihood under attack, and they took action. Three weeks after the fence went up, someone cut holes in it, directly in front of the doors of seven of the pavilions. The vandalism caused quite a stir. The railroad announced it was willing to spend $20,000 to find the guilty parties—and it patched the holes in the fence without delay. It hired detectives and stationed guards to protect the fence. The pavilion keepers were probably behind the gangs of suspicious young men who prowled the railroad right-of-way at night to intimidate the railroad's patrolmen.[30]

The uneasy situation continued until the beginning of 1904, when the park board agreed with the neighbors' petition and began the process of appraising and acquiring the midway land. This sliver of land was going to be expensive, and the owners—Vinette Lincoln (who was going through this whole process for the second time) and others—had declared they would not accept a low appraisal. When the report on the midway properties was filed in November 1903, it gave a valuation of about $10,000—divided so that about half would go to landowners, about 40 percent would go to the lessees, like William Poudler, and $1,300 would go to Irwin Gardner. Many of the landowners immediately objected.[31]

The park board still didn't have the funds to acquire the land. Over the previous two years, the board had dedicated time and money to create much of the Grand Rounds, condemning the parkland along West River Road and beginning to string together Minnehaha Boulevard from Lake Harriet to the falls. It had acquired the Godfrey Tract to begin squeezing out the businesses around Minnehaha. Given those expenses, the park board could not acquire new debt. The only way to raise the money for the midway land was to increase property taxes in the neighborhood.

The landowning neighbors around the falls were happy to pay, and by February 1, a few of the pavilion owners were giving their titles to the park board. The prices were ridiculously high. Land that was purchased in 1895 for $525 was sold to the park board nine years later for $1,600, and the landowners still complained that price was too low. In a sense, all the complaints and lawsuits from the 1889 park acquisition legal fight had had a good effect for Vinette Lincoln and the rest of the landowners. Whatever might have been the inflation of prices in the intervening years, people were given an extra six hundred dollars an acre over the 1889 offer. To everyone's surprise, Vinette conveyed to the park board lots 3–11 of Runyan's Addition. She did it from Penobscot, Maine, serving as the attorney for Bertha, who was still teaching in the Philippines. In the title, they insisted that the buildings on the property belonged to the Gardners. It was an unusual request: the landowner was thought to have owned the buildings, which is why Katherine Steele's request for the family house on the Godfrey tract was turned down. Surely Adelbert Gardner suggested that Vinette dictate these terms to the park board.[32]

The title transfer from Vinette Lincoln also insisted that rental payments would go to her and her daughters until the end of the Gardners' lease, which ran up to 1907. Another unusual request, since the park board would be the owner and ought to receive the rents. But perhaps they just did not want another protracted legal fight with Vinette.

During the 1904 season, the park board owned much of the land under the midway, but the battle was far from over. The fence between the railroad depot and the pavilions was still in place. Without any access to the midway from the Milwaukee Road, the pavilions turned themselves around to face Hiawatha Avenue. They took down their back walls and put in west-facing doors and windows. The *Journal*

The pavilion keepers turned their businesses around in 1904, building new entry-ways to the west, facing Hiawatha Avenue. *MNHS*

reported that a number of "new variety houses, refreshment stands, merry-go-rounds, and fakir's booths transformed Hiawatha Avenue into a Midway Plaisance where on Saturdays, Sundays, and holidays, people of a certain class make the day and night hideous. Unpleasant hilarity mars the otherwise peaceful beauty of the place."[33]

When Vinette secured the Gardners their midway income, they felt untouchable, so they, or somebody, upped the ante. On July 1, 1904, right before the important and lucrative July Fourth holiday, someone decided that the fence finally had to go. In the morning, neighborhood residents woke to find one hundred yards of fence posts had been sawn off, leaving large portions of the fence just lying on the ground. The destruction must have taken hours. Not every one of the resort owners was pleased by this act of aggression; the next day, an ad appeared in the paper: "Pavilion and extra ground space for sale cheap. Or will rent. Just the place for theatricals, tent show, dancing, or refreshments. Call quick."

Gardner's attorney notified the railroad that they were playing hardball. If the railroad put the pavilion-blocking fence back up, Gardner would sue the railroad to enforce a city law that required a six-foot fence along both sides of the miles of railroad right-of-way throughout the city, as well as gates and watchmen at every railroad crossing if the trains were moving faster than six miles per hour. The railroad stood down, and the fence was not repaired. The neighborhood residents determined to wait for the leases to expire, at which point Gardner's buildings would be removed and the park board could finally exercise its rights over the property.[34]

Some members from the Minnehaha Improvement Association began buying the land west of Hiawatha that was being colonized by the sideshows and refreshment stands. This was, they said, to prevent the pavilion menace from moving even closer to their homes.[35]

As the summer wore on, residents also stepped up their efforts to clear out the pavilions. They formed a vigilante committee and planned to deputize men to police the area and look for disorderly behavior, illegal booze, and grafters. Twenty women called on Mayor J. C. Haynes, asking him to shutter the rowdy establishments. Their complaints mentioned that there were late-night dances five nights a week, and they complained that on two nights, "colored people" were there. A former South High School football star named Charles Myrick had grown up to become the floor manager for these dances that welcomed the Black community. Myrick's father, Abraham, was born into slavery; after Emancipation he came north and took up barbering. His popular shop was in the West Hotel. An African American newspaper, *The Appeal,* spread the word about these social dances. And the women of the neighborhood complained that the noise was hideous, and that the area wasn't safe for them to traverse at night, on Sundays, or on holidays. The midway was between their homes and the streetcar and railroad tracks, so these women were unable to avoid the midway area, and for many reasons—including bigotry and fear—they were alarmed at the scene there.[36]

They made their case forcefully, and the next day, Police Chief Edward J. Conroy, who had largely been absent from the area, announced that Minnehaha must "be purged of its bold immorality, and gangs of hoodlums and roughs must be driven away." The police would "drive out creatures of both sexes who have converted Minnehaha into a place of reproach and shame." Conroy went through the midway, looking for signs of all the reproachful behavior he had heard about. He found nothing. The business owners, of course, knew he was coming, and they turned the music down and stopped the dancing. Even the red lemonade was a less riotous carmine, reported the *Minneapolis Journal*. The pavilion keepers got the result they were hoping for. Conroy reported that "the gathering at Minnehaha conducted themselves in a perfectly decorous manner. Nothing I saw could be construed as being disorderly or in violation of the law."[37]

The neighborhood's residents sank into despair. The pavilion owners must have been feeling cocky. And it was just six weeks later when Barnet's park board pavilion burned to the ground. A full investigation was expected, but the newspapers and everyone else immediately conflated the pavilion conflict with probable arson at Barnet's pavilion. As 1904 rolled to its close, the indictments against Irwin Gardner and Doc Ames were nolled, which means the prosecuting attorney went before a judge to say that he was satisfied that there would never be a conviction on these charges. With Irwin off the hook, and two more years on their lease, Adelbert Gardner was free to make money and a scene at Minnehaha.[38]

The park board commissioners turned their attention to the park and its surroundings. They had a serious problem with the park police sergeant, John F. O'Brien, who lived in the park and supervised Minnehaha's small police force. Because the pavilions were not inside the official park boundaries, policing the Minnehaha Midway was not the duty of the park police. But the troubles on the midway spilled into the park. At this time, the park board provided a house in the park for the park police sergeant. Sergeant O'Brien lived in that house, which was next to the Stevens House and near the western end of the bridge to the Soldiers' Home. O'Brien was a man of some influence, and hints of that show up in the park board's proceedings. For example, though his salary was seventy-five dollars a month, he presented a bill to the park board for two hundred dollars for "turning the water on and off." This was approved, then reconsidered and voted down the next month, on a six-to-three vote. Eventually, and more than once, he was given fifty dollars for this task. And this makes him a suspect in the questions about the water supply to Barnet's pavilion.[39]

The Stevens House, about 1903, just after the park board added protective fencing

Even worse, O'Brien had his own little graft operation going, which included shaking down couples who were canoodling in the bushes. Some of these people weren't even in the park, but when O'Brien threatened to arrest them, they paid with cash, boxes of cigars, or whatever else they could convince him to take.

In 1905, the scandal broke. O'Brien had been having parties—involving women and kegs of beer—at the Stevens House. Other policemen on the Minnehaha Park police force then provided evidence of more crimes. O'Brien faced a laundry list of charges: neglecting the animals in the zoo, shooting captive deer to eat at his keg party (which he dubbed the "Deer and Beer Party"), stealing fodder from the zoo for his cows, stealing building materials, allowing unlicensed vendors, firing employees who worked on the political campaigns of park board president Abraham Adams, and shaking down the public on threat of arrest. Even with this packed schedule, he also still managed to be charged with sleeping on the job.

SOMETHING ROTTEN AT MINNEHAHA.

They say the falls are beatiful, but the investigators of the Minnehaha park scandal go equipped thus.

A *Minneapolis Journal* editorial cartoon published April 17, 1905, reacted to the John F. O'Brien scandal.

Another park policeman named Burns testified that O'Brien claimed to have something on Parks Superintendent Berry: "He said he had Berry right where he wanted him." When Officer Burns volunteered to tell the park board committee what exactly it was that O'Brien held over Berry, however, the committee hastened to make it clear that the superintendent was not the one on trial. We may never know how Berry was being blackmailed, but he quit at the end of the season. O'Brien resigned as well, and in a controversial and frankly unsavory move, Abraham Adams, the former park board president, took his place on the park police force.[40]

The authorities began to tighten their grip. Mayor David P. Jones asked for a lockup to be built in the park; someone suggested it should be constructed from the burned pavilion's debris. Another plan, never carried through, was to construct jail cells in the basement of the new fireproof refectory. The mayor and the police intended to redeem Minnehaha from all of its boozy, lower-class shenanigans, and drunkenness in the area around the falls became a separate crime that came with mandatory jail time.

Mayor Jones made his intentions clear, saying: "A condition of absolute security for all visitors . . . will obtain, no matter if it requires dozens of police officers to secure it. . . . The idea that a handful of disreputable characters can defeat the purpose of thousands of respectable people in search of innocent recreation is monstrous. And it is as absurd as it is monstrous. There will be no such thing. The park will be made clean and inviting for the enjoyment of all the people. No half-hearted measures will be used. Order will prevail, not for one day in the week, but for every day. And Minnehaha Park during the season of 1905 will be as free from annoying features as Loring park. And the citizens can take my word for it."[41]

"The police say the tough element, excluded from the park, is determined to get even with the police," the *Journal* reported, "and they become intoxicated in order that trouble may be started. After this, money will not pay for their fun." Sentences of forty days in the workhouse were handed out to several men in June.[42]

Things seemed to be winding down at Minnehaha Park with all these efforts toward respectability. And then, after a four-year absence, Vinette Lincoln came back to town.

The return of Vinette Lincoln

Vinette Lincoln let the 1906 season play out. The Gardners finally gave up. In March of that year, they sold their lease on lots 3–11, Lincoln's former property, to a local dairy farmer named Martin Nelson. The park board authorized its secretary to demand that Nelson immediately vacate the land and that Gardner demolish or remove his buildings. Nothing is heard about this until October, when Nelson asked to have his lease canceled. This was referred to committee. All the while, the park board collected the lease money from Nelson and the pavilions that remained in Runyan's Addition.

In 1906, the police maintained a strong presence in the midway area. The city had given control over Minnehaha Avenue to the park board so they could enforce antipeddling rules along the street. Things remained pretty quiet. Perhaps Vinette was taking time to come up with her next scheme.

It wasn't until October that she made her move. She got an alderman to ask the city council to abandon the public easement for the Wenonah Triangle, a tiny triangular park of not quite a quarter of an acre, in the Lincoln Addition. The intersection of 42nd Avenue South and Hiawatha formed its northern tip. That little park (see map, page 116) had sat unnoticed and unused for sixteen years, ever since the Lincoln Addition had been platted. Lincoln reclaimed her little triangular park, making the argument that it had not transferred over to the park board because the board had never accepted it. When the park board heard that, it arranged to fence in the park. And Mrs. Lincoln, "not wanting trouble" (her lawyer claimed), sold the land to William Poudler. He immediately paid a man to live there, and then went to court with a quiet title suit.[43]

The park board's meeting proceedings are absolutely silent on all of this; the story comes from the newspapers. The neighborhood held a meeting and resolved to fight alongside the board to prevent another pavilion from going up. Eventually, Poudler lost his court case, and the park board took over ownership of the little park. More than a century later, the board sold the Wenonah Triangle to the city, which sold it to the person who lived next door to it. Vinette Lincoln went on to live at her cottage on Lake Minnetonka. The Gardners moved to Chicago, where Irwin became a successful doctor. William

A view along muddy Hiawatha Avenue in May 1907 showed that the midway was gone. *MNHS*

Poudler hung on the longest, running a small store and lunchroom at 4920 Hiawatha Avenue well into the 1920s—and nearly until the end of his life.

In May of 1907 the park board finally tore down the remains of the Minnehaha Midway. The month before, the park board had issued a permit for a peanut stand on park land at 50th Street. And a few days later, on the next piece of land to the west of the Wenonah Triangle, an ice cream stand was opened at East 49th and 42nd Avenue South, and plans were made to build a roller-skating rink and a dance hall next to it.[44]

8

The Neighborhood Responds

A FTER ALL THESE YEARS OF EFFORT, the neighborhood was obviously not quieting down. Far from it: In 1906, on the north bank of Minnehaha Creek, just across from all these rowdy businesses, a man named Robert F. "Fish" Jones bought a great piece of land from the children of Franklin Steele. It was at the bend in the creek west of the falls, where he moved his exotic animal menagerie out to the falls from its former Hennepin Avenue location. Jones took in the animals from the zoo in Minnehaha Park when it was closed. He also built the still-standing Longfellow House as his home.[1]

The name "Minnehaha Improvement Association" was revived in March 1906 by people in the neighborhood. The real estate people had moved on; Ed Runyan had gone to Oregon a few years before. These neighbors convened their association to address the concerns they had about the place they lived. They had no love for the Longfellow Gardens Zoo and the roaring of the lions that would continue for more than twenty years, but they never had the place shut down, either. Their immediate issue was to beautify the neighborhood by having children plant flowers and to urge people with cows to keep them from wandering. Before long, their focus shifted to weightier matters: the continued encroachment into the neighborhood by the businesses that catered to the fun-loving visitors to Minnehaha Falls.[2]

The midway was gone by May 7, when the association sent a contingent to tell the park board that giving a man named Blind John the concession to run a peanut stand was an affront that they would not assent to. Spokesman Sylvanus A. Stockwell made the honestly irrational argument that allowing this one stand meant that there was nothing to stop the park board from filling the former midway strip with pop booths or peanut stands all run by blind men. And the Improvement Association was not going to let the park board forget it.[3]

William Poudler bought the property at 4920 Hiawatha Avenue and in 1908 opened a store and lunch counter there. An ice cream stand went up at 49th Street and 42nd Avenue, built by Charles Snyder in 1907, and in 1908 Snyder built something called a "pavilion" on the same piece of land. There are a couple of newspaper mentions of a dance hall on the same corner, though there is no building permit for it.

The city council passed a dance hall ordinance in 1908, requiring that such places be licensed. The first version of the ordinance gave the permit to any who asked. But without an investigatory step, "the

William Poudler's refreshment stand at 4920 Hiawatha Avenue. *HHM*

ordinance as passed appears to be merely a provider of additional revenue to the city," noted the *Tribune*. Leaned on by the Women's Christian Temperance Union, the council realized that they needed to change the ordinance to require at least a bit of investigation into the merits of an application. Even considering the desired revenue, how could the city council approve a dance hall just a block west of where the Gardners had had such an inglorious setup?[4]

Snyder's "pavilion" was a roller-skating rink. (One might notice that dancing could happen in such a place.) It was also a clear indication that the problem of (and the demand for) rowdy hijinks would not go away. Of course, the neighborhood association had a tried-and-true way to stamp out this latest menace. They went to park board commissioner Edmund J. Phelps.

Obviously, this problem was not the park board's, just like the midway was not, and the activities on the Godfrey Strip were not; none of that happened on park land. But a few weeks after the roller-skating rink opened, the park board bowed to this pressure from district court judge Alexander Harrison and others. The board did something that utterly enraged the residents who lived nearby.

At the end of June 1908, the park board voted to close East 49th Street. It had a wire fence built on park land (in fact on the old Runyan's Addition) across East 49th Street where it crossed Hiawatha Avenue.[5]

When the Minnehaha Midway was torn down, the park board was delighted with its success. Members announced, "The theme of song and story, the shrine of visitors from every clime and nation is our own, our priceless and unapproached possession." They were also delighted that Minnehaha Avenue in front of the park was now graded and paved. What was called "the frequently impassable, crooked and water-logged old country road" was replaced by a modern paved boulevard forty feet wide with cement curbs and gutters.[6]

Pavement was scarce at this time in the far reaches of south Minneapolis. Most of the roads were dirt, which often meant mud; they were, indeed, frequently "impassable, crooked, and water-logged." And so, when the park board closed the road at 49th Street, it denied access to that new paved road to people who had moved into the falls neighborhood. The fence cut off easy access to both the streetcars and the Milwaukee depot. Those residents were obliged to go south around the fence, then back north, taking the long way around to reach

The *Minneapolis Tribune* of July 1, 1908, printed a blurry photo of the park board's fence across East 49th Street.

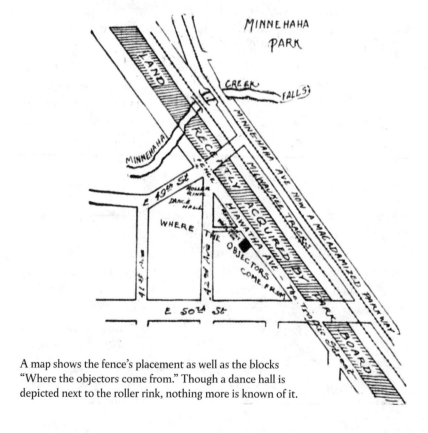

A map shows the fence's placement as well as the blocks "Where the objectors come from." Though a dance hall is depicted next to the roller rink, nothing more is known of it.

the streetcars. Some reports said that the neighbors could cross at East 50th Street, and other stories said that they had to walk down to 54th to go around the fence. Either way, the barrier of the fence was an unnecessary and unwelcome inconvenience. "Women and children found it necessary to wade through mud and water, over un-lighted streets, without sidewalks," reported the *Minneapolis Tribune*.[7]

Unsurprisingly, the people in the neighborhood went to the city council to complain. At the time, there were two aldermen for the Twelfth Ward. Aldermen Martin McHale and Willard W. Ehle checked with the city attorney, who said the park board had the right to block that road. The fence prevented people from crossing the newly acquired Runyan's Addition. The aldermen then used a city charter provision that authorized them to order removed any ob-structions to traffic. There was a street commission (because there was always a commission for everything in those days); the aldermen told the street commissioner to open the road. Accompanied by the unhappy people of 49th Street and the vicinity, on June 29, the street commissioner's crew cut the wires of the fence, and then they cut the posts down. Within a very short time the park board sent a crew over to repair the fence.

The neighbors called the park board's action arbitrary, unjust, un-necessary, and high-handed. But Alexander Harrison was still in there swinging *for* the fences, in his desire, as he said, for a respectable park. He and park superintendent Theodore Wirth and park board secre-tary James A. Ridgeway gave their view of the situation. They said that owners of objectionable places were given plenty of warning to move, but they refused. They said closing the road would inconvenience the customers of these places and would drive them out of business. It's not clear where they expected the businesses to move to; past actions from the park board and from the neighborhood association clearly show that they just wanted those businesses—however popular with fun-loving park goers—to be gone.[8]

· The neighborhood split. Unfortunately, this battle between the business owners and the neighborhood association power brokers (who were using the park board as their proxy) hurt the residents, the more than fifty families living west of the park for whom 49th Street was the most direct route to transportation to the city. East 49th Street had had some improvements recently, sidewalks and such; it was by far the best way to reach the streetcars. Other roads in the vicinity were often nearly impassable due to mud and water. Alderman Ehle predicted something would be done about the fence soon.

And then, in the early hours of the important and lucrative Fourth of July holiday, the roller-skating rink burned to the ground. The park policemen had been working in shifts that night, keeping a close eye on the repaired fence. The policeman on guard alerted Fred Swain, the night watchman who was in the building. It was 2 AM, but Swain couldn't sleep because of the mosquitoes. Swain managed to save two hundred pairs of roller skates in this by-now-expected but deeply foolish act of going back into a burning building.[9]

At this time, a fire station had just been opened at East 45th Street and Hiawatha Avenue. Minneapolis's first African American firefighting crew rushed to the scene. That fence-watching policeman refused to let them tear down the fence to reach the burning building.[10]

Superintendent Wirth later offered his written opinion to the park board that, even if the fence had not kept the firefighters from the fire, the roller-skating rink could not have been saved. The basis for this opinion is not known. He wasn't there.[11]

Everyone hoped this would solve the problem of the 49th Street fence, because the roller-skating rink was considered to be the cause. And because of that, everyone expected the fire was arson. But the people who benefited, the members of the neighborhood association, simply wanted *all* the amusements gone. William Poudler still had his lunch counter and small store, after all. Mayhem very likely could break out at any moment. The association passed a resolution in favor of the park board's fence, and they had that presented to the park board a few days later.

The fence stayed up.

One aftermath of the aldermen and neighbors having destroyed the fence in July was that the park policeman on the job was fired. Alderman Ehle said that there was no way the officer could have resisted the mob bent on destroying the fence, and that the fence was cut and the posts sawed down when the policeman went to get reinforcements. Alexander Harrison (now a former judge) took advantage of the moment to strongly claim that "90% of the residents in the neighborhood approve of what the board is doing, and are standing solidly with the park board. They want to see the undesirable pavilions driven from that part of the city. The aldermen are acting contrary to the wishes of the very people whom they profess to represent. Of this I am certain."[12]

Two days later, a resident of 49th Street rebutted all that in the newspapers. He said the 49th Street residents were "long controlled by two or three residents who have held various political offices . . . we are a unit for having the street opened," but these two or three politically powerful people "put the deal through in secret." The Improvement Association had been disbanded a couple of years back, said the writer; "if we have such a body, nobody knows who they are." And of course, the writer made the point that the closing of 49th Street inconvenienced people far more than it threatened the pavilions remaining just west of Hiawatha Avenue. To be effective, *all* streets would have to be closed.[13]

And that was a very good point. Why was this fence built, in this particular place, and why was it still standing after the reported menace, the roller-skating rink, had been burned? Less than two weeks after the fire, the *Tribune* had the answer. Even on July 10, they'd alluded to it. Judge Harrison, they said then, had "property interests in the neighborhood."

The *Tribune*, loyal defender of the conservative moneyed elite, ran a story that didn't exactly turn on Alexander Harrison, but it did kick him a little bit. Four years earlier, in 1904, some members of the Minnehaha Improvement Association bought some of the land west of Hiawatha that was being colonized by the sideshows and refreshment stands. They said it was to prevent the pavilion menace from moving closer to their homes. Turns out, they had a different plan.

Alexander Harrison and Frank B. Kidder had always been prominent voices in the pavilion fight. (Kidder had appealed to the park board to deny the peanut stand privilege to Blind John.) Living at 50th Street and 42nd Avenue and running a grocery on the next block was James R. Hartzell. He had testified against the Gardners' dance hall and the wild behavior he saw there (including drunken men shooting guns into the air). Hartzell ran the pony ride at the falls in some years; it was the very last of the amusements, and it lasted for generations. Harrison, Kidder, Hartzell, and a couple of others wanted to build a "beautiful hotel with spacious pavilion" on the land across from the park. After all they had done to extinguish the trade in accommodating park visitors, it is startling to believe they wanted to do this, but that was their plan, for the block of land between 49th and 50th Streets across Hiawatha Avenue from the former midway.[14]

Harrison said, "It is true that we have been thinking seriously of putting up a hotel. Under proper conditions, I see no reason why a hotel there should not prove a good investment. The plan has not matured into anything definite as yet, but the majority of the owners of lots there are agreed on working together in such an improvement or something similar. We have discussed also the construction of several cottages there for summer rental purposes but the presence of the pavilion now there, cutting up the block as it does, precludes our going ahead with any plans. We have offered to buy [Poudler's] pavilion property, but met with no success in the offer."

They owned almost the entire block, and they wanted to monetize their connection to the falls. Just like everybody else. William Poudler had bought the lot at 4920 Hiawatha just the year before for $350. Poudler had no intention of giving them the opportunity, nor of giving up his prime spot.

And in mid-July, the fence was again damaged and again repaired without delay. This time it was repaired with barbed wire. The fence got longer and taller with each repair. This was true in part because the park board realized that the fence had so few wires that people were going over or under them. But using barbed wire was just unnecessarily mean. The *Tribune* said, "the 'spiteful' barrier was bristling with wire stickers and radiating antipathy," and moreover, the fence was conveniently directing people right toward the very businesses it was meant to freeze out. Rather than walk to the streetcars down 49th Street, the fence forced people to walk past Poudler's lunch counter and store. The ice cream stand was having a wonderfully busy season. At least that proposed hotel was laid in an early grave. Harrison and the other promoters said it was only an idea, with no definite arrangements having been made. Perhaps they shied away from the idea due to the premature publicity.[15]

On August 2, 1908, the neighbors held a mass meeting at the fence, where all the "streeters" from along 49th Street gathered "to take such action as the citizens deemed just and right." The group drafted a petition to the park board, which was signed by three hundred people. The most prominent of the signers was the well-known artist

The park board used wire fencing in the park as well; this view may be from the 1890s. *Cooperative View Company, St. Paul*

Arthur Hurtt, who lived at 4830 39th Avenue South. The group, and in fact their petition, was entirely civil. But feelings were high, and three days later, an anonymous someone who was referred to as "Jack the Nipper" cut a person-sized hole in the fence.[16]

And that hole was, of course, mended the next day. Ignoring the petition, the park board reiterated its stand that all places of amusement in the vicinity should cease to exist and that the fence would stay until that happened. On August 10 a "furious raid" of angry neighbors took axes and nippers and tore down the ten strands of barbed-wire fence and threw it into the creek. The despised work of the park board was torn limb from limb.[17]

That was on a Saturday night. On Sunday morning, when Theodore

Wirth heard what had happened, he got in his car and drove to the homes of the eight park board workers whose job was to repair the fence. He insisted they get their tools, get in his car, and get that fence back up. And the fence was up again before the neighborhood returned from church.

The local politicians got involved again. Alderman Ehle invited the park board to come to the fence location and see how difficult it made life for the neighborhood. He asked about the petition, too, which had been "referred to committee." Policemen were still guarding the fence, and Ehle and some others tested the policemen's interest in following orders when the five of them climbed over the fence. The policemen declined to arrest the alderman, but did hand out fines on other occasions to fence climbers.[18]

In October, Sylvanus A. Stockwell returned to the fray at Minnehaha. He was running for alderman in the upcoming election, and he asked the park board to leave a person-sized hole in the fence so people could walk over to the streetcars. The street was largely still closed (wagons and buggies could not go that way), but people could get through the fence. Stockwell was a previous member of the Minnehaha Improvement Association, but he was motivated by controlling alcohol access and not by trying to starve out an ice cream stand or Poudler's lunch counter and small grocery. Stockwell was not one of the hotel builders, either; it seems he did this in order to promote his candidacy.[19]

Even though a small gate was installed in the fence, the neighborhood was not impressed by Stockwell's compromise solution. He wasn't elected. Instead, the fence stayed up and anger continued to simmer into the summer of 1909. It's not clear why this solution was insufficient. Probably it was a patchwork of sentiments held by different people: some wanted to drive their buggies over to the new macadam surface on Minnehaha Avenue, some were angered by Harrison and others trying to grab the land for their own project, and some still remembered the promise of easy transportation from 1887 with the fifteen-cent round-trip fares. Poudler sued the city and the park board for loss of business, inconvenience, and loss of stock of merchandise. He asked for about $6,000, and asked the judge to strike from the park board's answer all the complaints about rowdy dance halls, which Poudler was not running, and which in fact did not exist. He ultimately settled, accepting five hundred dollars for his losses.[20]

Months later, in August of 1909, the fence was torn down completely, though not by the park board. The eyewitness report said, "I was awakened by two shots fired. When I went to my window, I saw ninety men swarming about the fence with saws and wire cutters. One of them had a gun in his hand. Before you could say Jack Robinson, every man had two fenceposts under his arms. These were taken to Minnehaha Avenue and 49th Street where they were piled high in the air then someone poured a lot of oil of some kind on the fence rails and then applied a match. As the flames shot upward, I heard the crowd cheer and then they all left the place." The entire destruction happened in just twenty minutes. The two shots had been fired by William Poudler, who said later that he thought he had heard a prowler on his property. He might have; two cans of gasoline disappeared from his porch that night. And—surprising no one—not a single one of the neighbors who watched from their windows recognized anyone in the crowd. By this point, it was two hundred yards of fence.[21]

And the next day the park board rebuilt it again. Now the neighborhood had involved the city council members, the street commissioners, the mayor's office, the newspapers, and the public. They had written and submitted petitions. They had made their claims time and again about the inconvenience of having their route to transportation closed. And through it all, the majority of the park board dismissed their complaints. Commissioner Phelps took a paternalistic attitude. "We desire to accommodate the people," he said, "but they will never get anything any quicker by tearing down the fence." Commissioner Charles A. Nimocks had already made a motion to take the fence down, but the majority of the board sided with Phelps and, by extension, with Harrison, Stockwell, and the Minnehaha Improvement Association.[22]

The park board did attempt to devise a scheme where it could use hedges instead of fencing to direct traffic away from the pavilions, and this would allow the neighbors to reach the streetcars but make it harder for foot traffic to reach any places of amusement. Not, in the end, a workable solution. At that time, in late August 1909, the *Tribune* reported that the fence would come down soon.[23]

Arthur Hurtt, the artist, wrote a lengthy history of the situation in a letter to the editor of the *Tribune*. It was Hurtt who said that the few politically powerful people who were manipulating the park board had simply lied about there being a dance hall; he said they were angry at not being elected. It was impossible for Hurtt to sell his home due to the fence; he said that Poudler's confectionary was where neighborhood people went to buy milk and cream and that he was well liked. Hurtt announced that he was leaving Minnehaha for good and moving to California (which he did).[24]

It simply isn't clear why the fence stayed up after the rink fire, and after Poudler refused to be pressured into selling. There is no trace of alcohol-fueled rowdyism; that really was extinguished when the Gardners admitted defeat and left the falls. But the fence stayed up.

As 1909 wore on, a delegation of thirty people went to argue about this in front of the park board. Both sides were represented, one side arguing that the fence deterred dance halls and "music parlors," the other side railing against the injustices of the enforced long walk on muddy streets and their falling property values. The park board voted to leave the fence up. Stockwell was at that meeting (though he actually lived a long way away, at 3204 East 54th Street). J. R. Hartzell was there, too. But Judge Alexander Harrison wasn't. We don't know why he missed the meeting. But Judge Harrison does leave the story. He died in 1911, and the family sold the house and moved away to a smaller place.[25]

That fence stood there blocking 49th Street until 1912—so long that it was no longer news. Perhaps it was not a coincidence that Judge Harrison had just died. But after four years of trying to starve out William Poudler, the ice cream stand, and other little businesses, the park board quietly relented. The board took its fence down and reopened East 49th Street. Park Superintendent Wirth made the point: should any "objectionable business" attempt to set up across from Minnehaha Park, that fence would go right back up again.[26]

~

In 1914, a building was put up across from Vinette Lincoln's little triangular park at the corner of 49th Street and 42nd Avenue—that disputed piece of land where the roller-skating rink had burned down years before. It lasted until at least 1968. It had various names and

The OMNI Bar, 4900 42nd Avenue South, was photographed August 5, 1964, by Lyle F. Tieman for the Minnesota Department of Transportation. *HHM*

purposes over the years. During Prohibition, it was a beauty shop. It later became a tavern called the OMNI Bar, and when that closed, it was torn down. The land it sat on became the property of the park board. East 49th Street, which had once allowed people access to the park, was removed in the 1980s and made into more park land.

The little building had been owned by many people over the sixty years a business stood there. For decades, a family with the last name of Hoeffken owned it and ran it as a confectionery. And it is delightfully ironic that they lived in the house just off the corner of 50th Street on 39th Avenue, a house that is still standing, a house that was built by Judge Alexander M. Harrison.

Conclusion: Setting the Stage for the Modern Park

T HE NATIONAL ENERGY FOR ENDING legal sales of alcohol grew and grew during all the years of Minnehaha mayhem and during its slow demise. Just seven years after the 49th Street spite fence came down, Prohibition became the law of the land. The institutions of illegal alcohol and the attendant large-scale rowdyism left the park, and they have not returned.

In 1921, the park board began operating a Tourist Camp in the park, on the site of today's Wabun Picnic Area. Small cabins were available for rent to the new automobile tourists who ventured out of the cities onto the hard, rough roads of the countryside. By the thousands, people motored to Minneapolis, mostly from the Upper Midwest, but visitors were noted from all over the world. For three dollars a night, they could get a cabin with one or two beds, linens, a table, and electricity. The price was half that if they brought their own linens. By the mid-1950s, the camp was judged to be obsolete and was closed. The camp did not become a scene of notable drunken rowdyism. There were dances, even, but not calls for the paddy wagon to arrest illegal booze sellers.[1]

MUNICIPAL TOURIST CAMP
Minnehaha Park
MINNEAPOLIS, - MINN.

You are cordially invited to attend a Dance Entertainment at
"THE LOG CABIN"
Given for the Tourists of the Camp
8:00 P. M., SATURDAY, AUGUST 18
BOARD OF PARK COMMISSIONERS

The park board itself ran the last dance hall at Minnehaha. This small leaflet may have been distributed as late as 1951.

Some of the cabins in the Tourist Camp were built by the Works Progress Administration (WPA) in the late 1930s. This federal project helped people find employment and accomplish useful, necessary work during the Great Depression. WPA projects in Minnehaha Park in the 1930s and 1940s included maintaining the buildings like the 1892 picnic pavilion, planting trees and grass, and building the now-closed toilet building in the Deer Pen. WPA workers also built the long staircases that take visitors down to the creek level. These are in great need of repair today, after more than eighty years.[2]

The worst and frankly ruinous work from the WPA was the still-standing bridge over the creek just above the falls. That limestone bridge was built so that its footings are at creek side, and they are often in the water. This created a chute for the creek, narrowing the creek bed just above the waterfall.

When one compares the old pictures of Minnehaha Falls with the way it looks today, it's easy to see that Keating's "beautiful parabolic sheet" from 1823 was lost when this bridge was built. There have been several huge collapses of the Platteville limestone in the twenty-first century, and perhaps this chute effect is accelerating the erosion at the falls. Or perhaps the waterfall is naturally retreating upstream, as it has done for thousands of years.

The Old Soldiers' Home is now known as the Minnesota Veterans Home. The soliders' home commission members who wanted to place the home in an outstate town would probably be pleased that veterans homes have been built in Luverne, Fergus Falls, and Hastings. But the site on Godfrey's old claim is still going strong, offering skilled nursing and independent care for more than three hundred veterans. Though it seems new buildings go up all the time, a few of the nineteenth-century buildings are still in use.

After Prohibition, and indeed for more than a hundred years, the Minneapolis park board has offered hospitality at Minnehaha Park. Sometimes, they've operated the concessions directly; other times they've contracted to outside parties. By 2022, the Minnehaha refectory was home to Sea Salt Eatery. The original front of the refectory building has been modified, adding a nicely shaded patio where folks linger over lunch within earshot of the falls. The place is a strikingly successful operation. On pleasant summer days, the line to order fish tacos or oyster po'boys can mean a forty-five-minute wait, and more

Picnickers, about 1867. Unlike visitors today, these folks could have a bottle of beer as they sat beside the creek. *Photo by A. A. Palmer*

time before one's meal is served. People pass the time by getting a pint or a pitcher of beer and drinking as they wait in line with their friends. While this is a very lucrative endeavor for both the Sea Salt owners and the park board, it's not family-friendly. Little kids find it hard to wait so long for their meals.

The park board has also rescinded the public's right to bring and drink alcohol in the park. Currently, visitors may purchase the strong beer and wine available at Sea Salt, and they must consume it in the immediate area of the refectory. Until recently, 3.2 beer was permitted everywhere in Minnehaha Park, but that's no longer true. Bringing your own to your picnic is no longer tolerated without a permit applied for in advance, a certificate from the city, an insurance policy, and the hiring of two park police officers. These guidelines are obviously for large events, but there is no other provision for legally sipping some merlot with your picnic sandwich or downing a bottle of Corona while fishing below the falls.

This current situation at Minnehaha means a large crowd in a small space, nearly all of them adults, many of whom have had a couple of beers. It is the basic human equation for misbehavior and is in fact the exact situation Minnehaha has been in so many times over nearly two centuries. The possibilities for drama are tamped down by the daylight-only hours of the concession, the lack of opportunities to dance, and the generally well-behaved population.

But, who knows? Maybe there will be a time again when seedy shenanigans drive responsible people away from the lovely, laughing water. Ever since Longfellow put those words into his poem, many people have joked that the "laughing water" was whiskey.

Author's Note

"THE FUTURE HISTORIAN WHO TURNS his attention to Minnehaha Falls and the romantic surroundings will be able to write several separate and distinct chapters on the periods of its origin and development." The *Minneapolis Tribune* published that statement on May 12, 1889, and 126 long years later, I finally noticed it.

At that time, I had been that future historian of Minnehaha Falls for fifteen years. I'd studied the place for so long because I had this collection—thousands of images and souvenirs related to the falls.

Perhaps you have a collector's nature and you understand how it is. For us collectors, our attention gets caught by some thing, and we are overwhelmed by the desire to have it, and another like it, and to learn more about the things, and so on in what can be an obsession or A Grand Obsession. This depends on how much of one's time, attention, income, and home the collection consumes. Before long, you are hunting for, enjoying, learning about, and storing firecracker packages, or Chinese restaurant menus, or PEZ dispensers, or cuff links, or handmade hay bale hooks. After a while, you have a lot of these things.

I began collecting Minnehaha Falls items when I lived along Minnehaha Parkway in Minneapolis. The collection had a perfectly rational beginning. My overgrown garden needed some refreshing, and I wondered if there had been a historical planting plan—a design—for the parkway. While considering this, I found, on a bookstore shelf in a Smithsonian museum in Washington, DC, a substantial book titled *Regional Garden Design in the United States*. It contained papers from the 1991 Dumbarton Oaks Colloquium on the History of Landscape Architecture series, and I bought it when I found within a paper titled "Fast-Tracking Culture and Landscape: Horace William Shaler Cleveland and the Garden in the Midwest," written by University of Minnesota professor Lance Neckar. And here I began to learn the history of the Minneapolis parks system.

As it turned out, no plant list was integrated into the parkway

Another cooper's work at Minnehaha Falls. *Photo by Samuel P. Cox, ca. 1890*

design. I began looking for old materials that would show the plants in use at the time in Minneapolis, and that led to a few picture postcards of the creek. There are many more postcards of the falls than of the creek, and before long I was collecting those, and then I realized that nineteenth-century photographs of the falls were widely available. And so it went.

Today, my collection includes thousands of images and souvenirs. Archivists pay attention to the sort of historical flotsam I've accumulated. But the difference between an institutional, professional archivist and me is clear. Institutions attempt to collect a bit of every historic thing in their domain. I am not a broad collector but a deep one. The front garden at my house on the parkway got fixed up without referring to historical sources. And, in a true expression of that overused old chestnut, the rest is history.

It's actually easier to collect nineteenth-century photos than twentieth-century photos. That seems odd until you realize that the twentieth century was not so very long ago, and those pictures are still someone's cherished family photos. But when the last person dies who knew the people in the picture or where it was taken, or when no one is left who cares, that's when pictures come to the collector's market and I have a chance to buy them. Today, I have more than a thousand nineteenth-century photographs of Minnehaha Falls.

A collection of a thousand pictures of the exact same place: what possible use could that be? (Collectors with Grand Obsessions smile in empathy and never ask that question.) But mine is a curious nature, and so I began studying these images because I wanted to know which of them was oldest. This led me to studying early professional photographers, and I now can often tell which of those nineteenth-century photographers took the image just by looking at it.

Dedicated collectors tend not to lose their passion for the subject when their interests drill down into smaller and smaller facts. (PEZ collectors call this "the minutiae of the stem.") In my case, I found myself ignoring the waterfall in my Minnehaha picture collection. I began to look at the edges of the images, at the small structures hidden in the trees, the bridges built and washed away, footprints, broken branches, and graffiti. People were responsible for all of that, and naturally enough I wondered who, exactly, those people were.

The answer to that question is this book. As you've seen, I've studied Minnehaha as a scene of drunkenness, greed, arson, prostitution, blackmail, and lawsuits. But there's more (always more!) to the story, and those tales can be found on my website: urbancreek.com. Feel free to contact me and to share your Minnehaha stories and pictures; I learn so much from the people who know and love Minnehaha Park as much as I do.

Acknowledgments

T HIS BOOK IS A COPRODUCTION with the worldwide COVID-19 pandemic. Being locked down while writing sounds ideal on its face. And then one realizes that all of the collecting institutions whose original materials one might need to see are also in lockdown. Research—unless digitally available—became impossible. As restrictions began to lift (temporarily) in the late spring of 2021, and my deadline came racing toward me, the staff at the Minnesota History Center's Gale Library made endless small miracles happen. Michele Pollard, archivist at Hennepin History Museum, delighted me with images and stories that I didn't know existed. Ted Hathaway, Bailey Diers, and Jenna Jacobs at Hennepin County Library Special Collections could not have been more prompt and wonderfully helpful.

Writers will tell you that sitting down and putting the words on paper or on screen *is the job*. This is my first book, and I am here to say that that is, indeed, how it works. Writers will tell you support is also critical. Yep, that's true, too. In my case, major projects of deconstruction and construction at my house made writing at home impossible in the last three months before my deadline. I am so profoundly grateful for Joe Agee and Andrew Bertke, David and Shannon Perry, Larry Sanderson and Thong Dinh, all of whom offered me the bliss of quiet work space, gladdening conversation, snacks, and even sandwiches. John Crippen at Hennepin History Museum also provided writing space, and now that I've mentioned sandwiches might well have one of those for me, too.

David Perry and especially Adam Stemple gave me feedback. I learned so much from these talented writers sharing their expertise and pointing out ways the story could be even more interesting. Zac Farber, my editor from the *Southwest Journal* newspaper, gave me calm, detailed advice when I was stuck. Timothy McCall and Stefan Songstad had their own ways into parts of this tale, and we shared stories. In particular, Stefan found the Rascher insurance map, which helped quite a bit of Minnehaha's history snap into focus. Jim Sampson gave me some useful high-level editorial insight. Tom Trow shared his knowledge of archaeology and local history and gave me useful critiques at key points. Longfellow scholar Nick Basbanes gave me good feedback and words of encouragement; too, the staff at the Longfellow House in Cambridge, Massachusetts, opened their doors and their files to me. Harvard's Houghton Library gave me access to images and miles of microfilmed letters. Claire Boeke was a terrific assistant on several occasions. Much clarity came to my complicated first draft from the uplifting, energetic editor Michael Jauchen, who shared my excitement for this history right from the first sentence he read, even though he'd never heard of Minnehaha Falls before. Mike, I am indebted to you.

Thanks to everyone at brain.fm, to Brewster Kahle and the Internet Archive, and to the Self Journal team for the tools that kept me working, and to the British duo Slow Club for the frantic, gentle, wise music I played endlessly during the weeks when I rushed to finish the book.

In times of catastrophe—deconstruction, construction, pandemic— we should all know enough to look to the helpers. Laura Jean, Sharon Kahn, Geri Sullivan, and Michelene Verlautz let me lean on them at crucial moments. Betsy Stemple lent me her fierceness and clarity. John Ladwig provided clever perspective and some key details. Becca Leathers and Brittany Edwards inspired me with their excitement and curiosity. A more obscured but no less valuable cast of characters who kept me resourced through the process of writing amidst catastrophe includes Adriene, Anna, Briana, Joe, Karen, Mike, Riley, Ruth, and Sara.

Others who gave me good feedback, guided my thinking, taught me interesting things, or aided the work in some way include: Bill Herdle, John Kenrick, David C. Smith, Clark Hansen, Billy Selander and Nanci Langley, Cedar Phillips, Aaron Novodvorsky, Stuart Klipper, David Schroth, and Peter Sussman. I'm sure to realize, much too late and with great embarrassment, that I have missed some people, though I'll note B., who was there at the beginning but did not stay to see how it turned out.

Ann Regan is my editor at MNHS Press. I like to say of Ann that she chose me from the chorus line to star in the show. When she asked to buy my as-yet-unwritten manuscript, I could not have been more flabbergasted nor more elated. With her trust to bolster me, getting the book written became my central (indeed, very nearly my only) activity in the spring of 2021. Ann, thank you for your insight, wisdom, and patience, and for all the ways your editorial expertise made this book better. It has been an extraordinary journey, and I could not have done it without you.

Notes

Extensive research into local history stories means pulling together information from scraps of evidence that are both convoluted to cite and not particularly informative to subsequent researchers, who can locate them with reasonable ease. These footnotes do not generally include citations for information found in online genealogical resources, manuscript censuses, military records, building permits, property records, city directories, various digital image collections, and birth, death, and marriage records, and some of the other resources listed on the author's website at http://www.urbancreek .com/assets-and-comrades/.

Each year, the park board produced an annual and a set of proceedings. These are held in the Minneapolis Park and Recreation Board Records, Hennepin County Library Special Collections; links to many of the digital versions are available at http://www.urbancreek .com/assets-and-comrades/park-board-history-documents/. Citations have been shortened to Park Board Proceedings and *[Number] Park Board Annual, [date]*.

Abbreviations used in notes:

MNHS   Minnesota Historical Society
MJ   *Minneapolis Journal*
MT   *Minneapolis Tribune*
SPG   *St. Paul Globe*

Notes to Introduction: The Lay of the Land

1. For more on geology, here and below, see Richard Ojakangas, *Minnesota's Geology* (Minneapolis: University of Minnesota Press, 1982), 111, 119. An especially clear, detailed explanation of local river valleys, waterfalls, and changes over time can be found in Frederick W. Sardeson, *Geologic Atlas of the United States, Minneapolis–St. Paul, Folio 201* (Washington, DC: US Geological Survey, 1916).

2. The only clue about otters found thus far is their mention on the brass plate describing the Minnehaha Falls panorama at the Bell Museum in St. Paul. It's plausible that otters once lived in the creek, and one may suppose beavers and muskrats also did before the traders in the area would have provided good reason to take the pelts for trade.

3. Office of the State Archeologist, Minnesota Archaeological Site Forms 21HE386 (Minnehaha Site, Area D and Area E) and 21HE391 (Debris Field Site, Area G), both dated Jan. 2009–Apr. 29, 2010. On the number of mounds in the area, see Newton Horace Winchell, *Aborigines of Minnesota* (St. Paul: MNHS, 1911), 242–69.

4. "Most Powerful Medicine," video available at Bdote Memory Map, bdotememorymap.org.

5. Warren Upham, *Minnesota Place Names: A Geographic Encyclopedia* (St. Paul: MNHS Press, 2001), 236. A Dakota speaker recorded the pronunciation of mniġaġa at http://bdotememorymap.org/glossary/.

Notes to Chapter 1: "Westward the Jug of Empire Takes Its Way"

1. Martin Case, *The Relentless Business of Treaties: How Indigenous Land Became US Property* (St. Paul: MNHS Press, 2018), 5–6, 54–57. For general background on Fort Snelling, here and later in this chapter, see Hampton Smith, *Confluence: A History of Fort Snelling* (St. Paul: MNHS Press, 2021).

2. Case, *Relentless Business*, 39.

3. On price per gallon, see W. J. Rorabaugh, "Alcohol in America," *OAH Magazine of History* 6, no. 2 (Fall 1991): 17–19; for consumption statistics, see Daniel Okrent, *Last Call: The Rise and Fall of Prohibition* (New York: Scribner, 2010), 7–9. To put this in perspective, consider that the daily wage for a laborer in Massachusetts in 1810 was between $.50 and $1.33: C. Davidson Wright, "Comparative Wages, Prices, and Cost of Living," from the Sixteenth Annual Report of the Massachusetts Bureau of Statistics of Labor, for 1885, 53.

4. Smith, *Confluence*, 98; George Washington to William Buchanan, Aug. 20, 1777, Founders Online, National Archives, https://founders .archives.gov/documents/Washington/03-11-02-0011; Michael Mahr,

"'Half the Time Unfit for Duty': Alcoholism in the Civil War," National Museum of Civil War Medicine website, posted Sept. 2, 2021, https://www.civilwarmed.org/alcoholism/.

5. Lawrence Taliaferro, "Auto-biography of Major Lawrence Taliaferro, Written in 1864," *Collections of the Minnesota Historical Society* 6 (1894): 234 ("first murder"; Taliaferro wrote about himself in the third person); E. D. Neill, "Occurrences in and around Fort Snelling, from 1819 to 1840," *Collections of the Minnesota Historical Society* 2 (1889): 102–42 ("I beg"). Neill referenced the letter from Taliaferro to Leavenworth in many of his Minnesota history pieces. One can hardly open a work of his without finding it.

6. Maj. R. I. Holcombe, et al., *Compendium of History and Biography of Minneapolis and Hennepin County, Minnesota* (Chicago: Henry Taylor & Co., 1914), 45 (teacher), 60 (trader at Coldwater); Lea VanderVelde, *Mrs. Dred Scott: A Life on Slavery's Frontier* (New York: Oxford University Press, 2009), 58 (well liked).

7. Taliaferro, "Auto-biography," 41, says that Mary Ann Perry was "a celebrated *accoucheur*" [*sic*]. The spelling "Perry" is phonetic; Taliaferro had no talent for languages and relied on interpreters for all his decades as Indian agent. Abraham Perret raised cattle for the garrison, and on occasions when one was taken by Native people, Taliaferro said he reimbursed Perret promptly.

8. Mary Lethert Wingerd, *North Country: The Making of Minnesota* (Minneapolis: University of Minnesota Press, 2010), 91 ("whiskey is their god"); Barbara K. Luecke and John Luecke, *Snelling: Minnesota's First First Family* (Eagan, MN: Grenadier Publications, 1993), 149 ("our martial code"). The name Little Crow was used by a few generations of Dakota leaders, but the description of the man as "aged" suggests this is Little Crow I, who signed the Pike's Purchase treaty in 1805; he died in late 1833 or early 1834: Nancy Goodman and Robert Goodman, *Joseph R. Brown: Adventurer on the Minnesota Frontier, 1820–1849* (Rochester, MN: Lone Oak Press, 1996).

9. Committee on Military Affairs to House of Representatives, Feb. 8, 1830, American State Papers: Military Affairs, 275–76.

10. Here and in the next paragraph, see "Report on the Subject of Desertions," Jan. 25, 1830, American State Papers, 4:289. That word "toper" is an excellent old term, now fallen out of use, for a hard drinker or a drunkard. It rhymes with "roper" or "doper."

11. Barbara Ann Shadecker Adams, "Early Days at Red River Settlement, and Fort Snelling: Reminiscences of Ann Adams, 1821–1829," *Collections of the Minnesota Historical Society* 6 (1894): 95 ("Sometimes it seemed"), 97 ("convivial spells").

12. Adams, "Early Days," 107. Snelling, who suffered from chronic dysentery as well as (probably) alcoholism, left the fort in 1827, after dueling with a fellow officer; he traveled to Washington to defend the post's financial records, which could not be reconciled. He died in 1838: Smith, *Confluence,* 81–82.

13. George Catlin, *Letters and Notes on the Manners, Customs, and Condition of the North American Indians* (Philadelphia: Willis P. Hazard, 1857), 2:590–92; see also Theodore C. Blegen, "The 'Fashionable Tour' on the Upper Mississippi," *Minnesota History* 20, no. 4 (Dec. 1939): 377–96.

14. Edward D. Neill, "Fort Snelling, Minnesota, While in Command of Col. Josiah Snelling, Fifth Infantry," *Magazine of Western History* 8 (June–Aug. 1888): 171–80, 373–81.

15. Kathy Swenson of the National Park Service observed that military sources preferred "Brown's Falls," while civilian sources leaned toward "Little Falls." Bde Maka Ska was named for Secretary of War John C. Calhoun, who served from 1817 to 1825; he later became vice president, then a US senator, and he was an ardent defender of slavery: Upham, *Minnesota Place Names,* 236. Dakota citizens worked with the park board to use the Dakota name meaning "Lake White Earth." The change became official in 2018.

16. This account of Joe Brown in the following paragraphs relies on Goodman and Goodman, *Joseph R. Brown.* This exceptionally well-researched biography summarizes what we can know about Brown. The authors also note that the story about the camping trip is first told in John H. Stevens, *An Address, Giving the Early History of Hennepin County: Delivered before the Minneapolis Lyceum* (St. Anthony, MN: Northwestern Democrat of St. Anthony and Minneapolis, 1856). Stevens later published a much-expanded version: *Personal Recollections of Minnesota and Its People and Early History of Minneapolis* (Minneapolis: [Tribune Job Printing Co.], 1890).

17. Stevens, *An Address.*

18. The particular parcel of land that is under discussion here was actually first purchased by Ard Godfrey, who claimed the land in 1852 and paid for it in 1856. The Bureau of Land Management has the original land patent: https://glorecords.blm.gov/default.aspx. The Goodmans describe the idea that Brown had a claim at Minnehaha as "curious" and suggest that Brown may well have been the source of the story—while suggesting, too, that Brown may not have understood his legal rights regarding land claims: *Joseph R. Brown,* 64.

19. Goodman and Goodman, *Joseph R. Brown,* 90–91, 95, 99–100, 103–9.

20. Smith, *Confluence,* 105.

21. Smith, *Confluence,* 101–3.

22. Here and in the next six paragraphs, see Goodman and Goodman, *Joseph R. Brown*, 160–65. (Emerson also enslaved a man named Dred Scott, who was at the fort at the time: VanderVelde, *Mrs. Dred Scott*, 74.)

23. On Steele, here and in the next paragraph, see Edward D. Neill and J. Fletcher Williams, *History of Hennepin County and the City of Minneapolis, including the Explorers and Pioneers of Minnesota* (Minneapolis: North Star Publishing, 1881), 635–38 (biographical details), 1857 Minnesota manuscript census ("gentleman"); Holcombe, *Compendium of History and Biography of Minneapolis*, 52–53 (Taylor's Falls), 61 (claim at St. Anthony). Holcombe places James C. Mencke ("as daring as he was unscrupulous") as a claim jumper to Steele's St. Anthony claim.

24. Norma L. Wark, *Papers of Henry Hastings Sibley: Fur Trader, Politician, and General* (St. Paul: MNHS, 1968), xviii (Baker's death, McKenzie as executor). On McKenzie (also sometimes spelled MacKenzie) and the Chouteau family, see various mentions in Stan Hoig, *The Chouteaus: First Family of the Fur Trade* (Albuquerque: University of New Mexico Press, 2010); the business was a commission house known as Chouteau & McKenzie.

25. William Watts Folwell, *A History of Minnesota*, 4 vols. (St. Paul: MNHS, 1921–30) 4:197 (Pond brothers). Neill and Williams say that the Swiss missionaries named Gavin and Denton each lived in the house during a portion of 1839: *History of Hennepin County*, 111.

26. E. Sandford Seymour, *Sketches of Minnesota: The New England of the West: with Incidents of Travel in that Territory During the Summer of 1849* (New York: Harper & Bros., 1850), 13, 116.

27. Bruce White, "A New House Built of Stone: New Information on a Coldwater Landmark," Mar. 18, 2009, http://www.minnesotahistory .net/wptest/?p=821 (Taliaferro recorded the St. Louis Hotel in 1853); *Weekly Minnesotian* (St. Paul), July 23, 1853 ("newly enlarged"). Several accounting records in the Franklin Steele papers, 1839–1888, MNHS (box 2 [1853], box 3 [1855], and others) show costs and payments for Heidsieck champagne and peach brandy, and "2 cases Cabinet" which could, one supposes, be the German Riesling Kabinett. These are surely for the hotel guests and not for the military.

28. Minnesota Territory, Legislative Assembly, House of Representatives, *Journal of the House of Representatives during the Third Session of the Legislative Assembly of the Territory of Minnesota* (St. Paul: Owens & Moore, 1852), 133.

29. Stevens, *Personal Recollections*, 176–77 ("many of the citizens," Cloutier sued); Edward D. Neill, *The History of Minnesota: From the Earliest French Explorations to the Present Time* (Philadelphia: J. B. Lippincott & Co., 1858), 565, 578–79; see also *MT*, June 29, 1919.

30. Marvin R. O'Connell, *John Ireland and the American Catholic Church* (St. Paul: MNHS Press, 1988), 105.
31. Box 13, vol. 25, Steele papers.

NOTES TO CHAPTER 2: THE LONG TAIL OF LONGFELLOW

1. Robert Taft, *Photography and the American Scene: A Social History, 1839–1889* (1938; New York: Macmillan Co., 1942; New York: Dover Publications, 1964), 8.
2. Hesler told this story many times. It was reprinted and retold in photography trade publications, in newspapers, and in dozens of other places. See, for example, J. A. A. Burnquist, *Minnesota and Its People* (Chicago: S. J. Clarke Publishing Co., 1924), 2:74; Beaumont Newhall, "Minnesota Daguerreotypes," *Minnesota History* 34, no. 1 (Spring 1954): 32; "Alex Hesler," Smithsonian American Art Museum, https://americanart.si.edu/artist/alex-hesler-6689, attributed to Merry A. Foresta, *American Photographs: The First Century* (Washington, DC: National Museum of American Art with the Smithsonian Institution Press, 1996).
3. Here and below, see Alexander Hesler, "An account of the taking of the first picture of Minnehaha Falls in 1852 and its use by Henry Longfellow in writing Hiawatha, [188-?]," MNHS Collections. The letter was also reprinted in the *Minneapolis Tribune*, Oct. 17, 1920; the reprint notes that the letter responded to articles published in the *Pioneer Press* on Oct. 8 and 16, 1886.
4. The US Bureau of Land Management has records of these first land patents, which then are carried on by Hennepin County. Ard Godfrey, the millwright who came to Minnesota at Steele's request, also had a claim at Minnehaha, paid for on June 14, 1856. His claim included the fifty acres along the river and north of the creek where today stands the Minnesota Veterans Home, and which Stevens said had been Brown's claim: Isaac Atwater and John H. Stevens, *History of Minneapolis and Hennepin County, Minnesota* (New York: Munsell Publishing Co., 1895), 2:1137.
5. On Blakeley, see William J. Petersen, *Steamboating on the Upper Mississippi* (Iowa City: State Historical Society of Iowa, 1937; New York: Dover Publications, 1995), especially the note to the image found between pages 79 and 80.
6. Charles Fisk, "Reconstruction of Daily 1820–1872 Minneapolis–St. Paul, Minnesota Temperature Observations," master's thesis, University of Wisconsin-Madison, 1984 (climate records). A letter Hesler wrote on February 9, 1876, from Evanston, Illinois, was printed in *The Philadelphia Photographer* 13, no. 137 (Mar. 1976): 67: "In looking over your Lan-

tern Journeys, your description of Minnehaha falls reminds me of a fact not generally known, viz., Longfellow never saw those falls until long after he had written 'Hiawatha,' if indeed he has ever seen them. The whole thing was suggested to him, and description made by him from seeing daguerreotypes I made of the falls and surrounding country, in the summer of 1851, in the month of August; the most fearfully hot days I ever experienced. On the same day, I made views of St. Anthony's Falls and the country line west of the river where Minneapolis now stands, then a naked prairie. This, I don't suppose will in the least interest you, but I thought it no harm to mention the fact. A. Hesler."

7. Andrew R. Hilen, *The Letters of Henry Wadsworth Longfellow,* 6 vols. (Cambridge, MA: Belknap Press, 1967–72).

8. Robert Taft also doubted this claim of Hesler's: "Mrs. A. B. Hesler of Evanston, a daughter-in-law of Alexander Hesler, informs me that the letter written by Longfellow is not now in existence, probably being destroyed in the Chicago fire of 1871, although she has heard Hesler describe its contents many times. The autographed copy of Hiawatha is in Mrs. Hesler's possession, however. Not knowing the original wording of the Longfellow letter, it is difficult to decide how much the Hesler daguerreotype was responsible for Longfellow's original conception of the poem": Taft, *Photography and the American Scene,* 471n110.

9. These letters are published in Hilen, *Letters of Longfellow*; others are in the Charles Sumner Correspondence at Houghton Library, Harvard University.

10. R. C. Waterston, "Memoir of George Sumner," *Proceedings of the Massachusetts Historical Society* 18 (1880–81): 205 (return to United States); Journal of Henry Wadsworth Longfellow, draft transcription provided to the author by Longfellow House–Washington's Headquarters National Historic Site, Cambridge, MA, hereafter cited as Longfellow Journal (visits to Longfellow); Sumner Correspondence (August and September travels).

11. Sumner's presence in Wisconsin is demonstrated by a letter he wrote from Madison City on July 21, 1853, to the Pilgrim Society, expressing regrets on his inability to attend. The letter was reproduced in a newspaper of the day; an undated clipping is in the author's possession. A reference to the same letter is carried in the *Boston Evening Transcript,* Aug. 2, 1853. On Freeport, see Addison L. Fulwider, *The History of Stephenson County Illinois* (Chicago: S. J. Clarke Pub. Co., 1910), 195 (Freeport lecture).

12. *Official Catalogue of the New York Exhibition of the Industry of All Nations* (New York: George P. Putnam & Co., 1853), 52. Hesler also exhibited pictures of St. Anthony Falls and Galena, Illinois.

13. Hesler first mentioned Sumner in his letter to Blakely of October 1886. George Sumner died October 6, 1863; Charles Sumner died March 11, 1874; Longfellow died March 24, 1882; Whitney died January 20, 1886.

14. Christopher Lehman, *Slavery's Reach: Southern Slaveholders in the North Star State* (St. Paul: MNHS Press, 2019), 66–67, 71.

15. Here and in the following two paragraphs, see William J. Petersen, "The Grand Excursion of 1854," in Curtis C. and Elizabeth M. Roseman, *Grand Excursions on the Upper Mississippi River: Places, Landscapes, and Regional Identity after 1854* (Iowa City: University of Iowa Press, 2009). This piece is reprinted from Petersen, *Steamboating on the Upper Mississippi*, 271–86.

16. Conversation with Archives Specialist Kate Hanson Plass at the Longfellow House–Washington's Headquarters National Historic Site, Cambridge, MA; *New York Times,* June 8, 1854.

17. Longfellow used the pronunciation "He-awa-tha": see Jane King Hallberg, *Minnehaha Creek: Living Waters* (Minneapolis: Cityscapes Publishing Co., 1995), 93, which reprints a letter dated Nov. 12, 1897, from his daughter Alice M. Longfellow.

18. Longfellow Journal, May 26, 1854.

19. Longfellow Journal, Dec. 17, 1846. John Banvard painted this panorama. Panorama historian John Francis McDermott analyzed the rate of unwinding and viewing panorama scrolls against the scheduled time for viewing the exhibition and concludes that the three-mile claim is "a tall tale": see "Appendix A: The Length of the Panoramas," in John Francis McDermott, *The Lost Panoramas of the Mississippi* (Chicago: University of Chicago Press, 1958), 165.

20. Having visited the pipestone quarry, Catlin lent his name to, or imposed it on, the carvable soft red stone that is still quarried by Native people at the Pipestone National Monument near Pipestone, Minnesota. It is called both catlinite and pipestone.

21. Smith, *Confluence*, 113–14.

22. Mary Eastman, *Dahcotah, or, Life and Legends of the Sioux around Fort Snelling* (New York: J. Wiley, 1849), ii. Eastman was a southern woman who wrote a proslavery novel in response to Harriet Beecher Stowe's *Uncle Tom's Cabin*. She didn't limit her racial rancor to enslaved Black people; she also apparently disliked the Indigenous people she came in contact with. Writing in 1915 of her book *Dahcotah*, Henry A. Castle noted, "Mrs. Eastman disliked the Sioux and branded them as liars, thieves, and boasters; she also had the zeal of the evangelist in trying to supplant their paganism with a literal Christianity": Henry A. Castle, *Minnesota: Its Story and Biography* (Chicago: Lewis Publishing Co., 1915), 423.

Mary Eastman's animus toward the Dakota may have been exacerbated by her husband's history in the area. On his first tour of duty at Fort Snelling, Seth Eastman had married *a la façon du pays* Stands Sacred, a Dakota woman. He also supported and educated their daughter, Nancy Eastman: Smith, *Confluence*, 90.

23. Upham, *Minnesota Place Names*, 236.
24. Signe Alice Rooth, *Seeress of the Northland: Fredrika Bremer's American Journey 1849–1851* (Philadelphia: American Swedish Historical Foundation, 1955), 17, 19–20.
25. Rooth, *Seeress of the Northland*, 21.
26. Fredrika Bremer, *The Homes of the New World: Impressions of America* (New York: Harper & Bros., 1853), 13, 103, 123.
27. Longfellow Journal.
28. Bremer, *Homes of the New World*, 135. Longfellow also wrote about this dinner party in his journal.
29. Longfellow Journal, Jan. 23, Feb. 12, 1850; Bremer, *Homes of the New World*, 220. The plaster cast of Bremer's hand still exists in the collection of the Longfellow House–Washington's Headquarters National Historic Site in Cambridge. Fanny's letters, held by the Longfellow House, contain several instances of her describing how astonishingly petite Bremer's hands were.
30. Bremer, *Homes of the New World*, 2:19, 27, 54. Sibley was married to Franklin Steele's sister, Sarah Jane.

Notes to Chapter 3: Monetizing the Falls

1. *MJ*, Aug. 16, 1904.
2. Early property information—descriptions, sales, mortgages, deeds, and so forth—was recorded by hand in large books, and these records have been microfilmed. Hennepin County holds these microfilmed records at the Government Center, Minneapolis; hereafter cited as Hennepin County property records.
3. Smith, *Confluence*, 126.
4. Box 13, vol. 2 and vol. 6, Steele papers (owed money); *Weekly Minnesotian*, July 5, 1856, and Feb. 7, 1857 (lawsuits); box 4, business and correspondence records, Jan.–May 1857, Steele papers (note on lien). Box 1 (containing Miscellany Undated) of the Steele papers includes an undated note about buying the "Little Falls Property" of thirty-five acres and paying $125/acre. Please note that the "wildly complicated" claim in the text is not an exaggeration; it is an understatement.
5. Hennepin County property records show that some of the land at the Little Falls was owned by US Army Major Samuel Woods. Woods was married to Clayonia Barney, who was Annie Steele's sister. Clayonia

had four children, and three of them died with her of cholera at Fort Riley, Kansas, in 1855. They were interred "in the vault" on Steele's farm. When Lakewood Cemetery opened for burials in 1872, their remains were reinterred there. No burial vault exists in Minnehaha Park today. Box 1 (containing Miscellany Undated) of the Steele papers includes an undated receipt for work building the Minnehaha farmhouse and the vault and another for building a bridge below Minnehaha Falls. On dating the bridge below the falls, see Karen E. Cooper, "Transportation, Part 1," www.urbancreek.com/tag/first-bridge.

 Russell Fridley wrote that Steele "built a home at the northwest corner of the open acreage [outside the Fort]": "The Editor's Page," *Minnesota History* 42, no. 6 (Summer 1971): 232. This description does not preclude Steele building his house at the traffic circle location. As a counterpoint, Hennepin County property information lists the house, which is now at 5028 Hiawatha Avenue, as having been built in 1900. That's the date usually assigned to houses of unknown age. However, the real estate website Zillow claims (with unknown evidence) that the house was built in 1872, which squares with George Lincoln moving there after his house burned down—but not with the Steele story of construction before 1867. The early photographic record (see, for example, page 30) hints at a smaller house in the general location of the Steele house; it may have been added onto or even replaced. There just aren't clear records on it.

6. Here and in the following paragraph, see Rodney C. Loehr, "Franklin Steele, Frontier Businessman," *Minnesota History* 27, no. 4 (Dec. 1946): 309–18; Smith, *Confluence*, 132–35, 164. On Steele waiting to pay, see William W. Folwell, "The Sale of Fort Snelling, 1857," *Minnesota Historical Collections* 15 (1915): 404. Rice's letter to Steele is in box 4, business and correspondence papers, Jan.–May 1857, Steele papers.

7. Hennepin County property records.

8. Box 8, correspondence and business papers, 1867, Steele papers. There is a receipt for three thousand shingles for the roof of the "Saloon at Minnehaha," indicating that it needed repair. In the same year, the little bridge was rebuilt below the falls.

9. "St. Paul and the Cataracts of the Northwest," *The Friend Religious and Literary Journal* 41, no. 3 (Sept. 14, 1867): 19 ("homemade dinners"); *MT,* May 7, 1872, mentions that Geo. Boyden is running the place, but *MT,* June 4, 1872, says that Augustus Boyden ran those "first class accommodations."

10. *MT,* June 4, 1872. Hennepin County property records show that Steele quit-claimed the railroad right-of-way—a hundred-foot-wide strip—on October 31, 1863. The Steele papers contain scraps where Steele worked

out the costs of building the Cedar Valley road. It seems clear that the tracks ran right to Minnehaha Falls because Franklin Steele wanted them to.

11. *MT*, June 21, 1867.

12. Here and in the following three paragraphs, see Barbara J. Henning, *Historical Study Former U.S. Bureau of Mines Property Twin Cities Research Center* (Petersburg, IL: Rivercrest Associates, 2002), 17–18. On Lincoln, see George Lincoln to Franklin Steele, Dec. 1, 1861, box 6, correspondence and business papers, 1860–1861, Steele papers, for a letter, written on the letterhead of the Second Minnesota Regiment, that discusses George Lincoln providing rations and goods to the Union Army at Camp Anderson in 1861; and box 7, correspondence and business papers, Jan.–Apr. 1862, Steele papers, which contains a note to Steele from Lincoln placing him in this same activity at Camp Cumberland in February 1862. There are other similar letters.

13. *MT*, Mar. 23, 1871 (fire).

14. For the story of Captain Milo Palmer (and his son Albert), I am much indebted to conversation with Timothy McCall of the Friends of the Pioneers and Soldiers Cemetery and to his article, "Whoops They Did It Again . . ." *The Alley Newspaper* (Mar. 2016). *MT*, Feb. 9, 1872 (illuminated falls).

15. *MT*, Nov. 28, 1869. This story made national news.

16. *St. Cloud Journal*, Jan. 25, 1872 ($30,000); *MT*, Apr. 3, 1872 (work commenced); *MT*, May 7, 1872 (renovations); *MT*, June 4, 1872 ("Meals with all"). The Adams House was originally built by fur trader Philander Prescott.

17. *MT*, June 4, 1872.

18. *MT*, Feb. 13, 1873 (Merchants Hotel); *MT*, July 26, 1873 (leased the grounds); *MT*, Aug. 3, 1873 (takes possession "tomorrow"); *Kingston (NY) Daily Freeman*, Sept. 1, 1873 (cooked chicken). The lease was published in the "Abstract of Title to that part of the Fort Snelling Reservation Described . . . ," box 4, correspondence and business papers, Sept.–Dec. 1857, Steele papers.

19. *Catalogue of 6,300 Acres of Land to Be Sold at Public Auction, at Minne-Ha-Ha Falls: 1st and 2d Days of July 1873* (Minneapolis: Tribune Printing Co., 1873), copy at MNHS; see also *MT*, July 1, 2, 3, 1873.

20. Licenses were granted by the Hennepin County Board of Commissioners, but it respected the wishes of the local jurisdictions. See *MT*, Apr. 7, 1874 (Shaw license refused); *MT*, July 8, 1873 (Palmer license refused—yet his successor was given one on March 4, 1874); *MT*, Mar. 4, 1873 (Lincoln license granted); *MT*, May 5, 1874 (Richfield vote invalid).

21. *MT,* Jan. 3, 1874 (cocktails); *MT,* Aug. 29, 1874 (lease); *St. Cloud Journal,* Sept. 10, 1874 (foreclosure). According to the lease, Shaw had to pay only one hundred dollars a month for the first year at the Minnehaha Hotel. He still failed. He moved on to a hotel in Sioux Falls, South Dakota, that welcomed his expertise, but success eluded him there, too. He then tried prospecting for gold in the Black Hills—because why not—and eventually he found another hotel to run in Arkansas: *Bismarck Tribune,* Aug. 3, 1877.

22. *MT,* Oct. 27, 1874.

23. *MT,* Aug. 3, 1875 ("noticeable perfection"); *MT,* Nov. 23, 1875 (turkey shoot); *MT,* Jan. 21, 1876 (leap year party).

24. *MT,* June 14, 1876.

25. *MT,* May 17, 1871 (bathing rooms); *MT,* Sept. 17, 1872 (landlord complained). Henry was certainly born in France; every census agrees. That he may have been born in Alsace—the region on the border of France and Germany with a blend of Germanic and French cultural influences—seems likely, as the nickname "Dutch" is a corruption of "Deutsch," which, in German, means "German." Henry's daughter's obituary says he moved to Minneapolis in 1868, but he does not appear in the 1869 city directory. However, the 1868 and 1870 issues do not survive.

26. *MT,* June 8, 1875; *MT,* June 19, 1875.

27. *MT,* June 18, 1875.

28. In the 1880s, those soldiers included the Twenty-Fifth Regiment, a segregated all-Black unit: see Smith, *Confluence,* 165, 171, 173. On Henry's operations, see *SPG,* May 6, 1888 ("promiscuous gatherings"; the article is a retrospective written during the creation of the Soldiers' Home); *SPG,* Jan. 27, 1878 (Mendota farmer); *MT,* Aug. 5, 1878, and *SPG,* Aug. 7, 1878 (fights between soldiers and civilians); *MT,* May 15, 1878 (soldier stabbed); *SPG,* May 21, 1878 (military police).

29. *SPG,* Apr. 12, 13, 14, 1879. Johnson once hired a performing group consisting of a man named Charley Vincent along with Charley's wife and her sister, but the two ladies (one was married at sixteen; the other was just fifteen years old) refused "to go into the 'wine room' and entertain a lot of rough, intoxicated men." In response, Johnson docked almost a third of their weekly pay: *SPG,* May 13, 1879.

30. *MT,* May 16, 1879; see also *SPG,* May 16, 17, 1879.

31. Neill and Williams, *History of Hennepin County,* 216, 232. Another big grower at the time was R. J. Mendenhall, who had land just west of the falls and who would be a player in the Minnehaha Syndicate in the 1890s. Mendenhall's wife, Abby, was a social reformer out to rescue fallen women. Even though the Mendenhalls lived a life of such high

awareness of the disadvantaged, they also were from the antebellum South and had an enslaved Black child named Jerry in their household: Christopher P. Lehman, "Slaveholder Investment in Territorial Minnesota," *Minnesota History* 65, no. 7 (Fall 2017): 264–74.

32. *MT,* Apr. 29, 1873.

33. *MT,* May 23, 1875 (affordable flowers); *MT,* July 16, 1876 (summer houses, cool drinks); *MT,* July 16, 1877 ("unlimited flowers"); *MT,* June 28, 1879 ("Indian curiosities," "refreshments").

34. *SPG,* Aug. 29, 1879.

35. *MT,* June 10, 1878.

36. *SPG,* June 24, 1878.

37. *SPG,* Aug. 11, 1878.

38. *SPG,* Aug. 18, 1878.

39. *SPG,* Aug. 17, 1878 ("Gentlemen who understand"); *MT,* Aug. 15, 1878 ("minister"); *SPG,* Oct. 28, 1878 (drunks arrested). Donnelly advertised the reopening through April and May 1879; see, for example, *MT,* Apr. 24, 1879.

40. *SPG,* Apr. 13, 1879 ("Song and dance"); *SPG,* May 17, 1879 (Henry arraigned); *SPG,* May 30, 1879 (Donnelly charged, "Minnehaha never," and "no place"). On the musical moke, see, for example, "Frank Jones the Musical Moke," poster at the Library of Congress, https://www.loc.gov/item/2014637309/.

41. *MT,* June 23, 1879 ("just regaining"); *SPG,* July 31, 1879 ("sure knows").

42. *MT,* June 26, 1879, quoting Minnesota Statues 1866, Chapter C, Sec. 19.

43. *SPG,* Dec. 25, 1879 (brother died); *SPG* and *MT,* Jan. 17, 1880 (Donnelly to St. Paul, Booth lease).

44. *SPG,* Feb. 1, 1880. We don't know what a hurdy-gurdy swing was; it sounds noisy.

45. *MT,* Feb. 11, 1880.

46. *MT,* Mar. 16, 1880.

47. *MT,* May 28, 1880 ("to restore"); *MT,* May 17, 1880 ("scene of some"); *MT,* June 1, 1880 ("vulgar and profane").

48. *MT,* June 8, 1880.

49. *MT,* Sept. 9, 1880 (stricken); *MT,* Sept. 10, 1880 (Franklin's death); *SPG,* Jan. 14, 1881 (Annie's death); *MT,* Feb 1, 1881 (several million dollars). That the Steele children inherited becomes obvious as their land is taken for the park in 1889.

50. *MT,* Feb. 1, 1881 (Tapper at Minnehaha); Stevens, *Personal Recollections,* 108 (Tapper as ferryman). The Lincolns moved to land that he bought in Elliott's Second Addition within the "past three days": *MT,* Aug. 3, 1881. The address is reported in the 1881 Minneapolis city directory.

"Mrs. Capt. Tapper" was crushed to death in a sleighing accident; she lived at Minnehaha "upon the Franklin Steele estate" at the time: *MT,* Dec. 3, 1882.

51. The 1880 census listed names, race, and jobs for Booth's employees.

52. *Sixteenth Census of the United States, 1940, Population: Volume 1, Number of Inhabitants* (Washington, DC: Government Printing Office, 1942), 536; *First Park Board Annual, 1884,* 3.

Notes to Chapter 4: Four Long Years to Create a Park

1. *MT,* June 4, 1884.

2. Charles Eugene Flandrau, *Encyclopedia of Biography of Minnesota* (Chicago: Century Publishing, 1900) 152–57; Isaac Atwater, ed., *History of the City of Minneapolis, Minnesota* (New York: Munsell & Co., 1893), 2:599–602.

3. *SPG,* Aug. 30, 1887 ("Richer men"). A great glimpse into A. A. Ames's character is found in Erik Rivenes, *Dirty Doc Ames and the Scandal That Shook Minneapolis* (St. Paul: MNHS Press, 2018). The policeman Ames hunted with was his crony Charlie Hill, who is featured in Chapter 5.

4. Lincoln Steffens, *The Shame of the Cities* (New York: McClure, Phillips & Co., 1904), 65. The article on Minneapolis was first published as "The Shame of Minneapolis: The Rescue and Redemption of a City That Was Sold Out," *McClure's Magazine* (Jan. 1903).

5. *MT,* Mar. 5, 1885 ("saloon element"); *MT,* Mar. 13, 1884 ("His administration"); *MT,* Apr. 3, 1883 (one-hundred-dollar "low license"); *SPG,* Apr. 9, 1884 (number of saloons).

6. *SPG,* Apr. 9, 1884 (inaugural address); *SPG,* Apr. 24, 1884 ("refuse to grant").

7. "Hole in the wall" was another name for a blind pig. The *Oxford English Dictionary* finds "blind pig" in use in a Minnesota statute as early as 1887, though newspapers mention it earlier.

8. *MT,* May 2, 1883.

9. *MT,* July 31, 1884.

10. *MT,* July 31, Aug. 16, 1884.

11. Here and in the next paragraph, see *MT,* Feb. 26, 1868.

12. Mame Osteen, *Haven in the Heart of the City: The History of Lakewood Cemetery* (Minneapolis: Lakewood Cemetery, 1992), 25–26, 44; Lakewood History, Lakewood Cemetery website, https://www.lakewood cemetery.org/about/lakewood-history/.

13. This same sentiment could apply to *The Song of Hiawatha* itself. In the nineteenth century, it served as a stand-in for Native culture in the

minds of the many who didn't truly understand the devastation Indigenous people were being subjected to.

14. *MT*, Feb. 26, 1868.

15. This Union Park is not to be confused with the Union Park established in the 1890s by John Merriam and William Merriam, a few miles north in St. Paul: Bill Lindeke, *St. Paul: An Urban Biography* (St. Paul: MNHS Press, 2021), 51.

16. *MT*, Dec. 23, 1884 (resolution); *MT*, Dec. 17, 1884 (location debate).

17. *MT*, Dec. 24, 1884.

18. Here and in the next two paragraphs, see *MT*, Jan. 1, 1885 (Board of Trade legislation); *MT*, Jan. 23, 1885 (fairgrounds, capitol at Minnehaha). On railroad financing, see William Watts Folwell, "The Five Million Loan," *Collections of the Minnesota Historical Society* 15 (1915): 189–214.

19. *MT*, Mar. 7, 1885.

20. Here and in the following three paragraphs, see *MT*, Mar. 13, 1885 (commissioners appointed); *MT*, Apr. 3, 1885 (commissioners met); *MT, SPG*, June 25, 1885 (steamboat trip); David C. Smith, "Cleveland, Horace William Shaler (1814–1900)," MNopedia.org (Cleveland's influence). That Cleveland gets credit for designing the Grand Rounds leaves out the truth that he merely noted and enforced the tour of the beauty spots of south Minneapolis as all had done since people came here. Indigenous people's trails and pathways became the routes that settlers used. The Winchell Trail along the Mississippi in Minneapolis is the clearest extant example, but early maps show routes from the fort to the lakes. The very earliest written records of visitors talked of seeing the lakes, the fort, and the falls. What was called "The Drive of All Visitors" is not very different from the Grand Rounds: see Harriet E. Bishop, *Floral Home, or, First Years of Minnesota* (New York: Sheldon Blakeman & Co., 1857), 152.

21. *MT*, June 25, 1885 ("The use"); Alfred S. Dimond, *The Magic Northland* (Minneapolis: Hoppin, Palmer & Dimond, 1881), 82 ("Before the side").

22. *MT*, June 25, 1885 ("the falls which nature").

23. *SPG*, June 7, 1885.

24. *MT*, June 6, 1885 ("girl waiter"); *SPG*, Aug. 4, 1885 ("disorderly conduct"). For more on Collar, see Chapter 5.

25. *MT, SPG*, Dec. 2, 1885.

26. *MT*, Mar. 7, 21, 1886 (Pillsbury declines); *MT*, Mar. 24, 1886 (Pillsbury's consent); *SPG*, Apr. 2, 1886 (workingmen foreigners); *MT*, Mar. 28, 1886 (Ames corrupt, Pillsbury high license); *MT*, Apr. 7, 1886 (five thousand).

27. *SPG*, July 24, 1884 (crowd of 100,000).

28. *SPG*, Jan. 14, 1887 (GAR bill introduced); *SPG*, Mar. 22, 1887 (legislative appropriation); *SPG*, Apr. 1, 1887 (McGill); *SPG*, Jan. 2, 1887 (Congress). For locations toured, see *MT*, Apr. 13, 1887; *SPG*, June 7, 1887; and *SPG*, June 22, 1887.

29. *MT, SPG*, June 21, 1887.

30. *SPG*, June 2, 1887.

31. *SPG*, Jan. 24, 1887 ("back room device"); *MT*, Nov. 14, 1886 ("at present"); *MT*, Nov. 17, 1886 ("spoiling").

32. *SPG*, Mar. 1, 1887 ("In my opinion").

33. *SPG*, June 22, 1887 ("whatever is needed").

34. *SPG*, July 13, 1887.

35. *MT*, Aug. 18, 1887.

36. *SPG*, Aug. 9, 1887.

37. Here and in the next paragraph, see *MT*, Aug. 27, 1887; *SPG*, Sept. 8, 1887.

38. *SPG*, Sept. 10, 1887.

39. This phrase is printed on the deed: Hennepin County property records.

40. *SPG*, Sept. 10, 1887.

41. *MT*, Mar. 25, 1887 (lease advertised); *SPG*, Sept. 14, 1887 (rental authorized); *SPG*, Nov. 14, 1887 (vets housed).

42. *SPG*, Nov. 14, 1887 (greenhouse housing); *SPG*, May 6, 1888 (Booth's house housing); *MT*, Oct. 11, 1885 (Booth selling plants); *MT*, Jan. 7, 1887 (Booth's decline, foreclosure); *SPG*, Mar. 21, 1886 (drinking too much); *SPG*, Jan. 25, 1886 (death).

43. *SPG*, Nov. 15, 1887.

44. *SPG*, Jan. 9, 1887.

45. *MT*, Oct. 5, 1887 (supreme court cases); *MT, SPG*, Mar. 17, 1888 (lower court upheld).

46. *MT*, Feb. 18, 1889.

47. *MT*, Feb. 2, 1889.

48. Here and in the next paragraph, see *MT*, Feb. 6, 1889 (judiciary committee meeting); *SPG*, Feb. 6, 1889 (Vinette Lincoln and others); *SPG*, Feb. 13, 1889 ("It's robbery").

49. Here and in the next three paragraphs, see *MT*, Feb. 13, 1889.

50. Here and in the next paragraph, see *MT*, Mar. 13, 1889.

51. *MJ*, Jan. 21, 1906. Many years after the park was established, George Brackett spoke of public spiritedness and said that if the old guard had not pulled together, the permanence of Minnehaha Park would not have been assured: *MJ*, July 11, 1903. George Brackett's name continues at Brackett's Point on Lake Minnetonka, in Brackett Field Park in Minneapolis, and at Brackett's Trading Post, in Skagway, Alaska, where

he tried to build a wagon road to the gold strike in the Yukon, a wonderfully interesting story just beyond the reach of this book: see Julie Johnson, *A Wild Discouraging Mess: The History of the White Pass Unit of the Klondike Gold Rush National Historical Park* (Washington, DC: Government Printing Office, 2003), and Edwin C. Bearss and Bruce M. White, "George Brackett's Wagon Road: Minnesota Enterprise on a New Frontier," *Minnesota History* 45, no. 2 (Summer 1976): 42–57.

52. David Carpentier Smith, *City of Parks: The Story of Minneapolis Parks* (Minneapolis: Foundation for Minneapolis Parks, 2008), 46.

53. *SPG*, Sept. 4, 1887. George Lincoln died in 1883, but his oldest daughter, Bertha, sued her mother for her inheritance in 1887, when some details of the estate were published.

54. *SPG*, June 13, 1889 (minor irregularity); *SPG*, June 15, 1889 (Cox). These suits were undertaken after Vinette Lincoln had signed away the title but was trying to get her land back.

55. Hennepin County property records.

NOTES TO CHAPTER 5: THE SANDMAN OF MINNEHAHA FALLS

1. Much of the information in this chapter is based on the papers and belongings of Robert E. Fischer, which were given to the author by the estate of his granddaughters, Muriel Barrie and Marguerite Barrie. They received them from their mother, Edith Minnehaha Fischer Barrie; the materials were held by the family for more than seventy years.

2. *MT*, Mar. 4, 1888.

3. Edith's daughters told the author that their mother was born at Minnehaha. Their grandmother, Edith Totten Hoffman, was named for Fort Totten, where she was born. She was also the first white child to be baptized in today's North Dakota; Episcopal Bishop Henry Whipple did the honors. She used the same naming strategy for her first daughter. Another birth in the park occurred about June 1, 1953: Mrs. Shirley Meemken gave birth to a daughter in the Auto Tourist Camp. It seems certain that Indigenous children were born in the area before it became a park.

4. *SPG*, Aug. 13, 1891.

5. Here and in the next paragraph, see *SPG*, Mar. 12, 1889; Kris Manty, "Rare Sand Art by Andrew Clemens Sets World Record," Oct. 13, 2021, antiquetrader.com (sand art sale). Clemens's story is well told at the McGregor Historical Museum in McGregor, Iowa, which displays several of his sand art bottles as well as the tools he used to create them. MNHS has a dandy picture of the Hughes Drugstore in 1946 in its photo collection.

6. Here and in the next paragraph, see *MT*, June 16, 1889 (clean house). On

the legal battles, see Chapter 4; on Egbert Collar, see Foster Dunwiddie, "The Six Flouring Mills on Minnehaha Creek," *Minnesota History* 44, no. 5 (Spring 1975): 165; on Harriet Eves Collar, see *SPG*, June 18, 1889 (thirty minutes to vacate); *SPG*, June 20, 1889 (baby's death).

7. L. Mel Hyde was in Minneapolis from at least 1869; he worked as a painter and engraver, and by the mid-1870s he was involved with the Good Templars, a temperance organization. Harriet Collar probably did not serve alcohol in her restaurant.

8. *Minneapolis Star*, Sept. 17, 1927.

9. The story of the 200-Foot Strip is covered in Chapter 7. For Harriet's career as a sweet pea grower, see *MJ*, July 27, 1901.

10. *MT*, June 21, 1896 ("allowed the privilege" and suicide); *MT*, June 10, 1896 ("They say that").

11. *SPG*, June 8, 1897.

12. The gift to the author by Fischer's granddaughters included the remaining stock of these photos, as well as the glass plates themselves and quite a bit of Fischer's sand art.

13. *MJ*, Sept. 17, 1902 (1902 election); *MJ*, Aug. 19, 1902 (electric streetcar); *MJ*, Sept. 17, 1906, and *MT*, Sept. 3, 1912 (park board elections); *MT*, June 12, 1916 (ran for legislature).

14. *MT*, Nov. 5, 1914 (park board election); Park Board Proceedings, Apr. 7 and 21, 1915 (votes on sand art souvenirs). Fischer's granddaughters were quite certain that their mother Edith was never the sand artist.

15. *MT*, Aug. 7, 1919.

NOTES TO CHAPTER 6: MORALLY QUESTIONABLE PEOPLE HAVING FUN

1. *Eighth Park Board Annual, 1890*, 11 (picnic tables); *MJ*, July 19, 1902 ("Pride of Minneapolis"); Linda A. Cameron, "Twin City Rapid Transit Company and Electric Streetcars," MNopedia.org.

2. *MT*, Apr. 5, 1892.

3. Here and below, see *MT*, *SPG*, May 8, 1887 (low fares, planted trees); *SPG*, Apr. 24, 1887 ("other restrictive measures," 50th Street land donation). The restrictive measures were probably not racial covenants, as the Mapping Prejudice project (which has inspected thousands of Minneapolis deeds and mapped those with racial covenants) identifies a 1910 deed as the earliest of that type in Minneapolis; it also shows that properties on the north side of East Minnehaha Parkway and west of 28th Street were almost entirely restricted to white people only (see "What are Covenants" and maps at mappingprejudice.umn.edu). The Lake Amelia Outlots parcel is now included in park board property at Lake Nokomis.

4. *SPG*, Oct. 11, 1890 (Hiawatha opened).

5. *SPG*, Dec. 3, 1890; *MT*, Dec. 22, 1890.

6. The only picture yet found of people at Minnehaha in dissipated postures was used as the artwork on the cover of this book.

7. *SPG*, Apr. 20, 1897 (Reeves at pavilion); *SPG*, Oct. 2, 1887 ("fawn-eyed socialist"). The term was used consistently, for more than a decade, to describe Nymanover.

8. Frank G. O'Brien, *Minnesota Pioneer Sketches: From the Personal Recollections and Observations of a Pioneer Resident* (Minneapolis: H. H. S. Rowell, 1904); *MJ*, Sept. 4, 1904 ("a soft mark," "wholly unfit").

9. *MT*, Apr. 28, 1891 (building permit issued); May 15, 1892 ("souvenirs," "Ivey's").

10. William and Isabel Poudler had a son, William Fred, who (more or less) lived in his father's home at the pavilion. Poudler sued his wife for divorce on grounds of desertion: see *MJ*, Mar. 7, 1901.

11. *MT*, Aug. 6, 1895.

12. *MT*, Oct. 11, 1892.

13. *SPG*, Dec. 27, 1886.

14. *The Great West*, Aug. 15, 1890 ("sneak"); Apr. 11, 1890 ("deceptive genius").

15. On the African Dodger, see Jim Crow Museum, Ferris State University, Big Rapids, MI, https://www.ferris.edu/HTMLS/news/jimcrow/question/2012/october.htm. The *Tribune* also refers to "a frame of dolls"; they were likely dolls depicting a Black family, another typical target offered at carnivals at the time.

16. *MT*, *SPG*, Aug. 15, 1895.

17. *SPG*, June 8, 1897 (arrests); *MT*, June 19, 1897 (court fines).

18. *MT*, June 28, 29, 30, 1899; *SPG*, June 30, 1897.

Notes to Chapter 7: Corruption Reigns

1. Ames's career is discussed in detail in Rivenes, *Dirty Doc Ames*.

2. Rivenes, *Dirty Doc Ames*, 86.

3. Rivenes, *Dirty Doc Ames*, 96.

4. *MJ*, July 13, 1903 ("destroyed"); *MT*, July 18, 1903 ("violating").

5. Here and in the next paragraph, see *MT*, July 27, 1903.

6. *MT*, Feb. 16, 1913 ("had a truck farm," "the Sunday School").

7. For example, see *MJ*, July 13, 1901.

8. *MJ*, Dec. 14, 1904. After five trials, the remaining indictments were dropped.

9. *MJ*, Sept. 10, 1901 (Vinette and Fanny travel); *MJ*, July 13, 1901 (Bertha to Philippines).

10. Here and in the next three paragraphs, see discussions carried out through 1902 and 1903 in Park Board Proceedings.

11. *MJ*, May 25, 1903.

12. *MJ*, May 27, 1903.

13. Godfrey Parkway—also called the Godfrey Road and, before that, the Town Road—originated with Ard Godfrey's claim on the peninsula where the creek meets the river. The Town Road was opened in 1860 when Franklin Steele lived in his house at the falls; his papers include a mention of fencing off his property from the road: see Henry Reynolds to Franklin Steele, June 19, 1860, box 6, correspondence and business papers, 1860–1861, Steele papers. The road provided access for materials to be moved to and from Godfrey's saw and grain mills on the creek. It once led from the peninsula down to creek level, passed the old mill site, and continued on to the river. This section of the road gave easy access to the landing Ard Godfrey built on the Mississippi. Today, that road (the Lower Glen trail) is used by most of the people who walk from the falls to the river, by park maintenance staff—and, less often, by park police responding to unseemly behavior.

It has been more than a century since the Godfrey Tract was added to Minnehaha. The park board could have moved the parkway to the north side of the strip, allowing the land to become more fully incorporated into the rest of the park. But that has never happened.

14. Park Board Proceedings, Oct. 6, 1902 (Katherine [Steele] Appleby request). In an interview, Patten, the Sunday School Carnival Man, described the animals on his property: *MT*, Feb. 16, 1913.

15. *MJ*, May 25, 1903.

16. Here and in the next paragraph, see *MT*, July 8, 1903. The Midway pavilion owners began this campaign against the park board and its pavilion after the fence went up blocking access to their businesses.

17. *Twenty-First Park Board Annual, 1903*, 7.

18. Franklyn Curtiss-Wedge, *The History of Mower County, Illustrated* (Chicago: H. C. Cooper, Jr., & Co., 1911), 463 (cheesemaker); *Tenth Biennial Report of the Minnesota State Dairy and Food Commissioner* (Minneapolis: Great Western Printing Co., 1905).

19. *MJ*, July 31, 1903 (claret); *SPG*, Aug. 5, 1902 (Gardner resigned).

20. *MJ*, Aug. 4, 1904 (water supply, commissioners). On the gasoline engine, which was first provided by the park board in 1902, see *MJ*, June 10, 1903, June 21, 1904, and Nov. 8, 1904.

21. Park Board Proceedings, July 20, 1903.

22. *MJ*, May 13, 17, 1904.

23. *MJ*, Oct. 28, 1904 (fire); *MT*, Oct. 28, 1904 (kerosene, firefighters).

24. *MT*, Mar. 26, 1905.

25. *MT*, May 2, 1905 (winning bid); *Minneapolis Star*, Dec. 24, 1958 (nearly ninety, first movie theater); July 16, 22, 23, 1905, and Aug. 14, 1905 (falls illuminated).

26. *MT,* Jan. 21, 1904. Former state senator Sylvanus A. Stockwell pointed out that the streetcar would soon be extended to Fort Snelling and the soldiers would then have an even easier time getting to Minnehaha for some rowdy mayhem.

27. *MJ, SPG,* Feb. 3, 1903; *MT, SPG,* Feb. 4, 1903.

28. *MJ,* June 24, 1903 (on Gardner's property); *MJ, MT,* June 25, 1903 ("highway by prescription"); *MT,* June 30, 1903 (affidavits from neighbors, fence went up).

29. Here and in the next paragraph, see *MJ,* July 13, 1903 ("On Sundays").

30. *MJ,* July 20, 1903 (holes cut); *SPG,* July 21, 1903 ($20,000).

31. *MT, MJ,* Nov. 20, 1903 (appraisals; also Jan. 21, 22, 1904); *MT,* Dec. 8, 13, 1903 (objected).

32. *MJ,* Jan. 21, 1904 (happy to pay); *MT,* Feb. 9, 25, 1904 (lots purchased). Hennepin County property records has the sale records, including Vinette's location in Maine.

33. *MJ,* July 1, 1904.

34. *MJ,* July 23, 1904.

35. *MJ,* July 25, 1904.

36. *MJ,* Aug. 15, 1904 ("colored people" and complaints); *The Appeal* (St. Paul and Minneapolis), July 2, 1904 (Myrick).

37. *MJ,* Aug. 16, 1904 ("be purged," "drive out"); *MJ,* Aug. 17, 1904 ("the gathering").

38. *SPG,* Dec. 15, 1904 (nolled). Irwin turned state's evidence, testified against Doc Ames, and had his indictments dropped. This was also the case with Charlie Hill.

39. The John H. Stevens House, built in 1849–50 beside the Falls of St. Anthony (where the Minneapolis Post Office now stands, on South First Street) was hailed as the first authorized house built west of the Mississippi in what would become Minneapolis. This acclamation ignored the homes built by missionaries at Bde Maka Ska—but none of them survived. The Stevens House was moved to the park in 1896 and was placed near the end of the Soldiers' Home bridge. In 1983, the house was moved north to its present location and returned to historical accuracy, in a wonderfully sensitive restoration by the Minneapolis Junior League and historical architect Foster Dunwiddie.

40. *MT, SPG, MJ,* Apr. 12, 1905 ("He said he had").

41. *MT,* Apr. 20, 1905 (lockup); *MT,* Apr. 19, 1905 ("A condition of").

42. *MJ,* June 21, 1905 ("The police say").

43. Here and in the next paragraph, see *MJ,* Nov. 4, 1906 (abandon easement); *MJ,* Nov. 21, 1906 (sold to Poudler); *MT* Nov. 22, 1906 (quiet title, residents object).

44. *MT,* May 5, 1907 (torn down, peanut stand). The building permit for the ice cream stand was issued on May 13, 1907, and the permit for the pavilion on the same piece of land was issued on April 27, 1908.

NOTES TO CHAPTER 8: THE NEIGHBORHOOD RESPONDS

1. The zoo was open by June 1907. It is an endlessly repeated story that this Longfellow House in Minneapolis is a replica of Longfellow's home in Cambridge, Massachusetts. Sometimes, the claim is that it is a three-quarters scale—or a two-thirds scale—replica. The origin for this claim has not turned up, but it is *not true.* The author has toured both houses. There is a superficial similarity and a center-hall staircase inside the main door, but otherwise, nothing about the interiors is similar. The exterior appearance of Jones's house is clearly modeled on Longfellow's home, but it is not any sort of replica.

2. *MJ,* Mar. 18, 1906.

3. *MT,* May 7, 1907 (Stockwell and others complain); Park Board Proceedings, Apr.–Dec. 1907 (wherein we learn that Blind John's last name was Dunn).

4. *MT,* Apr. 21, 1908.

5. *MT,* June 30, 1908.

6. Park board president Jesse E. Northrup included these remarks in his President's Report in the *Twenty-Fifth Park Board Annual, 1907.* The waterlogged road being graded and paved was mentioned in Theodore Wirth's Superintendent's Report in the same publication.

7. Here and in the next paragraph, see *MT,* June 30, 1908.

8. Here and in the next paragraph, see *MT,* July 1, 1908.

9. *MT,* July 4, 5, 1908. The various reports do not make it clear who was running this business. One mentions "Green," probably someone named "C. S. Green," about whom nothing more is known; another claims that the person running the place was named Wendler. A seventeen-year-old newsboy named Sobelman tried to hire musicians at the falls. Where they were to play is not clear, but his age and background show that this was not a serious establishment.

10. *Star Tribune,* Dec. 7, 2020.

11. Here and in the next paragraph, see *MT,* July 7, 1908.

12. *MT,* July 10, 1908.

13. *MT,* July 12, 1908.

14. Here and in the next paragraph, see *MT,* July 15, 1908.

15. *MT,* July 22, 1908 ("the 'spiteful' barrier").

16. *MT,* July 29, 1908 ("to take such action"); *MT,* Aug. 5, 1908 ("Jack the Nipper").

17. Here and in the next paragraph, *MT*, Aug. 10, 1908 ("furious").
18. *MT*, Aug. 25, 1908 (invited); *MT*, Sept. 10, 1908 (climbed over).
19. *MT*, Oct. 10, 1908.
20. *MT*, Jan. 29, 1909.
21. *MT*, Aug. 21, 1909.
22. *MT*, Aug. 25, 1909.
23. *MT*, Aug. 24, 25, 1909.
24. *MT*, Aug. 29, 1909.
25. *MT*, Sept. 4, 1909 (thirty people); *MT*, Oct. 23, 1911 (Harrison house for sale).
26. *MT*, Aug. 26, 1912.

NOTES TO CONCLUSION: SETTING THE STAGE FOR THE MODERN PARK

1. Karen E. Cooper, "Category: The Tourist Camp," parts 1 and 2, http://www.urbancreek.com.
2. Karen E. Cooper, "Category: WPA Works at Minnehaha Park," http://www.urbancreek.com/category/wpa/.

NOTES TO SIDEBARS

i., page 11 American State Papers, 4:85–86.

ii., page 14 William H. Keating, *Narrative of an Expedition to the Source of St. Peter's River, Lake Winnepeek, Lake of the Woods, &c., performed in the year 1823, . . . under the command of Stephen H. Long* (Philadelphia: H. C. Carey & I. Lea, 1824), 302–3.

iii., page 16. John H. Bliss, "Reminiscences of Fort Snelling," *Collections of the Minnesota Historical Society* 6 (1894): 336.

iv., page 26 Taft, *Photography and the American Scene*, 6–8.

v., page 79 Charlotte Ouisconsin Van Cleve, *"Three Score Years and Ten": Life-Long Memories of Fort Snelling, Minnesota, and Other Parts of the West* (Minneapolis: Harrison and Smith, 1888), 40–41. Van Cleve was a leading Minnesota suffragist and the first woman elected to the Minneapolis school board. She founded the Bethany Home for "fallen women" with Abby Mendenhall and others.

vi., page 113 *Twelfth Park Board Annual, 1894*, 40, notes that "Two deer were added, making a herd of three"; an enclosure "50 feet square" was built for them. The list of animals in the zoo was extensively reported in park board annuals. The *Seventeenth Park Board Annual, 1899*, 42, reported these zoo residents, including "fowls and birds" from Loring Park and Lake of the Isles: 1 moose, 9 elk, 27 deer, 1 antelope, 4 black bear, 1 cinnamon bear, 38 rabbits, 1 alligator, 1 ape, 1 dwarf monkey, 1 gray squirrel, 1 black squirrel, 10 swans, 16 wild geese, 45 ducks,

1 mountain lion, 2 sea lions, 2 timber wolves, 3 red foxes, 1 silver gray fox, 4 raccoons, 2 badgers, 1 wild cat, 5 guinea pigs, 1 eagle, 4 owls, 5 peacocks, 6 guinea hens, 1 blue macaw, 1 red macaw, 2 cockatoos. Wirth began his campaign against the zoo in his first weeks on the job: *MT,* Feb. 6, 1906. On pony rides, see the history written by David C. Smith available on the Minnehaha Regional Park page at https://www.minneapolisparks.org.

vii., page 118 The list was included in a lease on his pavilion that Robert Fischer gave to a woman named Laura Martin; it is in the Fischer materials in the author's possession.

Index

Page numbers in *italics* indicate illustrations.